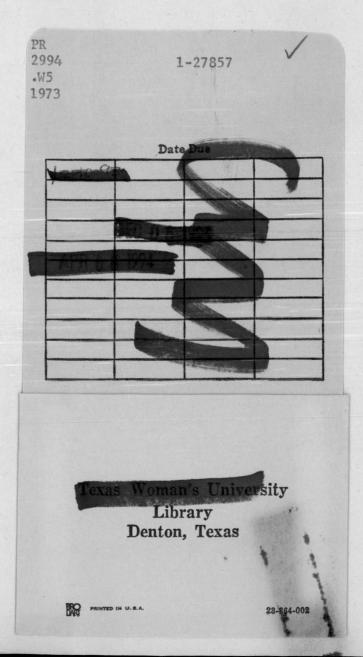

TO
  MILDRED

ALSO BY THE AUTHOR
  England's Eliza
  Prince Henry and English Literature
  editor of
  I. O.'s *The Lamentation of Troy for the
    Death of Hector*

SHAKESPEARE, SANTAYANA, AND THE COMIC

by
Elkin Calhoun Wilson

THE UNIVERSITY OF ALABAMA PRESS
University, Alabama
GEORGE ALLEN & UNWIN LTD
London

ACKNOWLEDGMENTS

Permission is gratefully acknowledged to the publishers and holders of copyright, here designated, for the use of material from George Santayana's *Soliloquies in England and Later Soliloquies, The Genteel Tradition at Bay, Character and Opinion in the United States,* and *The Realm of Essence* (all published by Charles Scribner's Sons); from H. B. Charlton's *Shakespearian Comedy* (Methuen & Co., Ltd.); from David Worcester's *The Art of Satire* (Eloise Worcester Spencer Wade); from E. K. Chambers' *Shakespeare: A Survey* (Sidgwick & Jackson, Ltd.); and from E. C. Wilson's "Polonius in the Round" in *Shakespeare Quarterly* (The Folger Shakespeare Library) and his "Falstaff—Clown and Man," in *Studies in the English Renaissance Drama* (New York University).

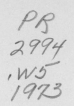
PREFACE

The common reader to whom this study is primarily addressed is happily free to ignore yet another book about Shakespearean comedy, although the weary scholar must pigeonhole it—while Thalia may laugh outright in tones far from silvery. I hasten to propitiate all. No mere mortal can pluck the heart out of the mystery of an immortal muse. My aim is with any cultivated reader to glimpse her better in the vestments that she wore when Shakespeare had his vision of her. Of both I seek to tell things not so new as true and, perhaps, not hitherto put within convenient compass.

Some years ago it occurred to me that certain areas in the writings of George Santayana give a secure foothold for a further view of Shakespeare and the comic insofar as that philosopher's naturalism looks more with amusement at life than beyond it and finds that in its "intrinsic aspect existence is nothing tragic or sad, but rather something joyful, hearty, and merry." I have quoted Santayana freely lest paraphrasing distort him. Of course I have pondered various views of the comic—physiological, psychological, and philosophical—taken by eminent inquirers of the past and present. Often I have followed inevitably in their footsteps. I try to bow duly to them as well as to numerous students who have lighted up this and that aspect of Shakespeare's comedies. I quote frequently from standard studies, but the ground has been too much tilled for one to recognize always the gardeners. Sometimes my perceptive students have enlightened their teacher. If I have seen anything not clearly beheld already, it is because I have profited from many quarters.

No one knows exactly which play Shakespeare wrote first, but students do agree as to what plays are early and what are late. In this study approximate dating suffices. Sources and textual matters are usually of secondary concern. Ideally, my interest embraces all manifestations of the comic angle on life within all the plays; but I am perforce selective in my illustrations from them, particularly when I face the later ones. The tone and the import of the comic strains in the comedies from *The Comedy of Errors* through *Twelfth Night,* not their structures, are the primary interest. Other comedies and the histories and the tragedies I give but limited attention, though I hope it is representative.

The notes, primarily documentary, often supplement the text for the interested reader. I quote from *The Complete Works of Shakespeare,* ed. G. L. Kittredge (Boston, 1936).

The reader who perseveres through the abstractions of the first chapter, concerned with definitions, will find chapters freighted with illustrative detail. The last chapter is not intended as a tract for our troubled times, but as a link between them and the comic as it is "embalmed and treasured up" in Santayana's comment on it and Shakespeare's way with it.

For various kindnesses, all very genuine, I wish to thank Phyllis Bartlett, Charles F. Beckingham, Elizabeth Brock, Douglas Bush, James G. McManaway, and Charles F. Zukoski, Jr. Three other friends, the late Albert S. Borgman, Daniel Cory, and Garrett Mattingly, encouraged this study. New York University gave me generously of sabbatical time. The dedication to my wife will suggest the measure of her helpfulness.

Birmingham, Alabama   E. C. W.
February, 1973

CONTENTS

I. PROLOGUE: On the COMIC and its KIN   1

II. The RADICALLY COMIC DOMINANT:
The Comedy of Errors, The Taming of the Shrew,
and *The Merry Wives of Windsor*   35

III. The COMIC and the ROMANTIC
INTERMINGLED: *The Two Gentlemen of Verona*   46

IV. The COMIC and the ROMANTIC
INTEGRATED: From *Love's Labour's Lost*
through *The Tempest*   56

V. The COMIC UNCONFINED: FALSTAFF   125

VI. The COMIC and the TRAGIC: *Hamlet*   133

VII. EPILOGUE   147

NOTES   158

INDEX   186

CHAPTER I

PROLOGUE:
On the COMIC and its KIN

Readers of Shakespeare know that the thirty-six plays in the First Folio edition in 1623 were grouped by John Heminges and Henry Condell, his fellow actors and first editors, as comedies, histories, and tragedies. They know, too, that there is comedy throughout those tragedies and histories—that Shakespeare did not respect the genres as did Aeschylus and Aristophanes and Racine and Molière. Juliet's nurse, two gravediggers, and a drunken porter make us laugh in the midst of tragedy. A supreme fool so jests with Lear in his agony as somehow both to relieve it and underscore it. The early *Titus Andronicus* is a tragedy so gory that it turns farcical for some tastes. Falstaff reigns as king of the comic in two histories; Pistol swaggers and rants in two. The capacious spirit of Prospero, dominating a great comedy as the First Folio designates plays, is no stranger to the tragic sense of life. If, thinking to better the classification by Shakespeare's fellows, we label romances or tragicomedies those late plays that followed the "dark" comedies and the major tragedies, Autolycus, Trinculo, and Stephano are no less laughable for the new terminology. What in common have folk so various—and so variously placed—as Launce and Viola, Mercutio and

1

Shallow, Enobarbus and Bardolph, Puck and Doll Tear-sheet, Rosalind and Dame Quickly? The linkings in such a partial roll call are themselves comic. What angle on life reveals such creatures? What rationale underlies them? Such large questions defy absolute answers.

Perplexity in any effort to describe Shakespeare's apprehension of the comic is not eased by the discordant voices of many celebrated critics of its nature. Does any term in literary criticism remain more a problem child in spite of having been lately psychoanalyzed? We speak glibly of this and that kind of comedy—low comedy, high comedy, realistic comedy, free comedy, satirical comedy, great comedy, burlesque comedy, farce comedy, literary comedy, comedy of wit, comedy of humours, comedy of manners, and (nowadays) "black" comedy—and so on and on, becoming ourselves, perhaps, more comical in so doing than Polonius in his subdividing of things dramatic.[1] Well may the skeptic doubt that anything so mobile and mutable as the comic has an identifiable essence.

When we turn inevitably to the Greeks for guidance we soon find Plato and Aristotle fathering the two classic concepts of the comic: the incongruous producing an emotional shock, surprise, or contrast that breeds laughter by suddenly disappointing our expectations; and the ludicrous, defined by Aristotle as some defect or ugliness that is not painful or destructive, evoking laughter as an outlet for scorn and derision before something inferior. The author of the *Tractatus Coislinianus*, Cicero, and Quintilian distinguish between laughter arising from diction and laughter arising from things; and the latter two see it stemming from a feeling of superiority or from deceived expectation. Such guidance from great ancients has illuminated most formal comedy since their days. It leads with varying emphases through Renaissance Italy, France, and England into Jonson, Hobbes, Dryden, Meredith, Bergson, and Shaw. Ben Jonson, who confronts us as soon as we face Shakespeare, commits his comedy to

> deedes, and language, such as men doe vse:
> And persons, such as *Comœdie* would chuse,
> When she would shew an Image of the times,
> And sport with humane follies, not with crimes.[2]

But the sporting line is very faint between the crimes and the follies of Volpone and Subtle. Jonson's Asper declares:

> Ile strip the ragged follies of the time,
> Naked, as at their birth: . . .
> . . . and with a whip of steele,
> Print wounding lashes in their yron ribs.[3]

Shades of Persius and Juvenal appear—the comic has turned into the satiric. Dryden, Shadwell, Congreve, Wycherley, Vanbrugh, and their fellows echoed one strain in Jonson's resounding voice that had pronounced comedy "a thing throughout pleasant, and ridiculous, and accommodated to the correction of manners."[4] After that irate moralist Jeremy Collier clubbed the lot of Restoration dramatic wits onto the defensive, almost all avowed anew moral ends for comedy. Molière had seen comedy as moral and corrective: "the use of comedy is to correct the vices of men."[5] This orthodox view of comedy as a social corrective to cure excess and mend manners by laughter Meredith inherited and gave his particular accent: comedy with the "sword of common sense" is the "guardian of our civil fort"; its "silvery laughter" checks deviations from the polite norm in highly civilized society wherein cultivated and charming women are its favorite tools for rebuking male egoists.[6] Subsequently Bergson wrote: "In laughter we always find an unavowed intention to humiliate, and consequently to correct our neighbour, if not in his will, at least in his deed."[7] Clearly a venerable lot of critics have found comedy essentially a social corrective that aims by laughter, springing from a sense of the incongruous or derisive, to hold men up to a norm of rational conduct even as tragedy would, many assert, recall them to it by showing what spectacles for pity and terror they become when they egotistically strut beyond it to disaster. Plato and Aristotle stand in the remote background of all such concepts of comedy as critical and corrective.

But if life is thus real and earnest for comedy in the hands of Jonson and many of his forebears and descendants, what of the sheer joy of it, its riotous and irresponsible fun that ignores all moral and didactic intents from Aristophanes (in good part) on? What of medieval folk comedy, of fabliaux—those "tales more broad than long"? What of much of Chaucer and Rabelais? Of Dickens and Mark Twain? Of Puck and Sir Toby, or Falstaff and Autolycus? What, in short, of

> Sport that wrinkled Care derides,
> And Laughter holding both his sides?

When comedy reopened shop in England in 1660 with the return of Charles II and his gay court from France, anger and indignation before vice and folly did vent themselves in various satirical forms; but the best stage comedy was, however corrective its professed intent, essentially naturalistic, witty, and hedonic.[8] Voltaire, who knew a lot about critical comedy and even more of its close kinsman satire and could happily wed them, yet declared that "laughter arises from a gaiety of disposition, absolutely incompatible with contempt and indignation."[9] Those feelings are involved in Jonson's critical comedy and are the life blood of traditional satire. Much laughter turns, surely, on the merely amusing, has no "unavowed intention to humiliate," is laughter of contagion, not of such "sudden glory" in superiority over one's faulty fellows as Hobbes wrote of.[10] Puck may exclaim "What fools these mortals be!" but his creator usually cries "What fools we mortals be!" to breed sheer merriment in the moment, relaxing and invigorating. Perhaps it is this particular touch of the comic spirit that most quickly makes the whole world kin.

Truth to tell, however, we do laugh in so many keys before so many things that we may well despair of ever extracting the greatest common denominator of all things comic. And yet, pondering this fact, one may suspect that point of view in time is primary for apprehending the comic aspect of anything. Our formal styles of yesteryear and stances struck in earnest then are laughable today—as our family photograph albums remind us. The world of Proust, as his contemplative eye ranged free in time from his tragic enmeshment in it, took on a marvelously comic hue. Again, does not the carefree laughter of our children, particularly at our sedate adult world, suggest that an innate, irresponsible play instinct underlies the comic? In such large matters, perhaps a little child should lead us.

For students of the comic, the child is indeed father of the man. One seeking its essence must probe the child's laughter to the quick; for in his discovery of the comic any child repeats man's evolutionary development of it. The underside of free and simple laughter remains, as we all know, a nervous phenomenon that agreeably releases bodily tension; witness our behavior when we are tickled in the ribs. About it, the physiologist may command the last word.[11] Even so, what tickles the playful child to laughter is the cornerstone of my inquiry. I at once recognize that the partition between his laughter and his tears is very thin, as parents know all too well. Do we not ourselves, like children, sometimes laugh until we cry—even cry until we laugh, if, alas, less often? Perhaps tears and laughter alike simply release or rest the same nervous system from unsupportable emotional tension. Here, possibly, is Shakespeare's footing when he mingles the comic and the tragic with unique power. This concern leads to the frontiers of my study, though it may well be remembered when we meet a moment in Shakespeare so poignantly poised between the pathetic and the ludicrous that we scarcely know whether to laugh or to cry—the one, for instance, in which Dame Quickly reports Falstaff's death.

Beneath any normal child's laughter is health, unfettered animal spirits, freedom from pain and care. Spontaneously curious and ready for any eventuality, he greets playfully whatever datum swims into his ken as it varies harmlessly from its immediate setting. He looks little before and less after, and his free and healthy response to the innocently novel radiates in smiles and laughter. So it is when he kicks and beams and clutches after a new toy dangled over his cradle; and so it is later when he romps with his playfellows in a new game. His laughter is still primarily animal exuberance, bubbling health like that in his puppy frisking around his feet. Such playfulness easily runs into sportive mimicry of his playmates—even of his dog's barking—for a histrionic instinct is his inheritance. A frightening false-face delights him if he knows his father's familiar one is behind it; and shortly he himself will be donning and doffing the thing to the terrified delight of his playmates. When this instinct in the child discovers the circus clown's mimicry, grimaces, antics, all in quick contrast with the sedate doings of his commonplace elders, the child responds with delighted laughter. D. H. Lawrence's hot rebuke to flat modern men who have lost their fellowship with the free play of animal life in a circus (and the world) need not deflect us from his awareness that children before the "bright wild circus flesh" are not without a sense of unity with that life—and laugh freely before it:

> Yet the strange, almost frightened shout of delight that
>   comes now and then from the children
> shows that the children vaguely know how cheated they
>   are of their birthright
> in the bright wild circus flesh.[12]

The tickled child, buoyant with health, untroubled by care, and utterly absorbed by any momentary capers cut by the clown, is our immediate progenitor as we keep a comic sense. His free fun in the immediate displays to us the delicious absurdity of all events as they flash before untroubled consciousness when we, become again somewhat as little children, catch them in nascent relief against the social conventions that usually blind us to their arbitrary nature after the shades of the prison house have closed upon the children that we were.

Now sometimes, as Santayana knew, "in the exuberance of animal life a spirit of riot and frolic" may come atavistically over the man fathered by that child; then he "leaps, he dances, he tumbles head over heels, he grins, shouts, or leers, possibly he pretends to go to pieces suddenly, and blubbers like a child. A moment later he may look up wreathed in smiles, and hugely pleased about nothing. All this he does hysterically, without any reason, by a sort of mad inspiration and irresistible impulse." He has become a child again just for the nonce. And this child-like man may go on to play the clown, that "primitive comedian"; he "may easily . . . turn his absolute histrionic impulse, his pure fooling, into mimicry of anything or anybody that at the moment happens to impress his senses; he will crow like a cock, simper like a young lady, or reel like a drunkard." What the child does spontaneously in jumping behind the mask to the fact and playing with both, your man turned professional clown does consciously and deliberately, to entertain and amuse an audience.

> Such mimicry is virtual mockery, because the actor is able to revert from those assumed attitudes to his natural self; whilst his models, as he thinks, have no natural self save that imitable attitude, and can never disown it; . . . He sees everything in caricature, because he sees the surface only, with the lucid innocence of a child; and all these grotesque personages stimulate him, not to moral sympathy, nor to any consideration of their fate, but rather to boisterous sallies,

as the rush of a crowd, or the hue and cry of a hunt, or
the contortions of a jumping-jack might stimulate him. He
is not at all amused intellectually; he is not rendered wiser
or tenderer by knowing the predicaments into which people
inevitably fall; he is merely excited, flushed, and challenged
by an absurd spectacle. Of course this rush and suasion of
mere existence must never fail on the stage, nor in any art;
it is to the drama what the hypnotizing stone block is to
the statue, or shouts and rhythmic breathing to the bard;
but such primary magical influences may be qualified by
reflection, and then rational and semi-tragic unities will super-
vene. When this happens the histrionic impulse creates the
idyl or the tragic chorus; henceforth the muse of reflection
follows in the train of Dionysus, and the revel or the rude
farce passes into humane comedy.[13]

Those celebrants of Dionysus, recapturing childhood's
freedom more easily than we do, abandoned themselves
to whatever wild animal impulses welled up into their
consciousness, quickened and driven by a riotous delight
in the clash of their doings with their backgrounds in
convention and propriety. Mimicry, mockery, sportive
playfulness marked their mad ecstacy. Humane comedy
evolves, as Santayana indicates, from this healthy animal
surrender to the immediate, delight in its denial of all
that a social order imposes. But humane comedy mingles
reflective overtones with such irresponsible animal revel-
ry; it has become acquainted with the grief of mere mortals,
caught and confused in the fatal web that existence over
times weaves upon the loom of infinite being; and it
introduces structure and design. Yet all that is truly comic
keeps as its core this irresponsible, pristine playfulness
in the extant moment. It never wholly loses its sense of
the riotous flux of the momentarily existential in absurd
contrast with the static and the conventional, however
dignified they may be, however precious to moral life
spread over time.

Formal comedy as early as we can discern it in literary
history is already "humane comedy" in which "the muse
of reflection follows in the train of Dionysus"; yet such

comedy throughout its long life has freely reverted to the "revel or rude farce" that in folk festivals, carnivals, circus clowns, puppet shows, and slapstick still delights children and simple folk—and refreshes folk not so simple. Such was the life blood of the *commedia dell'arte;* it pulses in the improvisation of any good clown of yesterday or today, in his intimate give and take with his audience. Such atavism in humane comedy exposes the taproot of the comic in the sportive play of healthy spontaneous life, enormously amused by the absurd contrast between onrushing existence and encrusting convention. It is forever slipping in children and clowns into mimicry as their innocent or squinting eyes focus momentarily on our social postures, always laughably at odds with our basic animal impulses.

Santayana's hand has led us rapidly, if securely, I think, from the clown's childlike perception of the radically comic into the highlands of humane comedy; and we have caught a glimpse of the midlands of the satiric and the valleys of the tragic that stretch around all. Into these realms one inevitably moves in tracing the comic in Shakespeare's capacious art. We may well pause even now for a sweeping bird's-eye view of the total landscape of which the domain of the comic is one province.

Thin partitions indeed divide the comic from the tragic.[14] To live in the world we do separate the day from the night; but in some locales light and darkness merge very subtly—there is a land of the midnight sun. Although we all know sun-up from sun-down and tears from laughter, truth to tell, the "head is not more native to the heart" than the comic is to the tragic. Everyone has heard Horace Walpole's assertion that "the world is a comedy to those who think, and a tragedy to those who feel," and Byron's cry: "And if I laugh at any mortal thing / 'Tis that I may not weep." The too neat dichotomy in Walpole's dictum is obvious. What is the world to a "feeling mind"? To a "thinking heart"? Housman and Keats struck old truth in asserting that " if men think they fasten / Their hands upon their hearts" in a world "where but to think is to be full of sorrow." Significant, however, is the involvement of only one world in Walpole's observation. Actually, this one "universe changes its hues like the chameleon, not at random but in a fashion which moral optics can determine, as it appears in one perspective or another; for everything in nature is lyrical in its ideal essence, tragic in its fate, and comic in its existence." Mature eyes catch such a threefold view of "everything in nature": a lyrical when we take things purely as eternal essences disclosed to intuition; a tragic when we feel them on our pulses as fatally implicated in time and space; and a comic when in the extant moment we face them as things with something of childhood's playful delight in the irrational, kaleidoscopic flux of life caught on the wing. For an adult sense of the comic, this "world is contingency and absurdity incarnate, the oddest of possibilities masquerading momentarily as a fact." And for "anything to emerge from that twilight region" of "unheard melodies and uncreated worlds" is indeed "inexplicable and comic, like the popping up of Jack-in-the-box; and the shock will amuse us, if our wits are as nimble as nature and as quick as time."[15]

Our wits are, alas, too seldom so. Life for even the most rational animal is primarily a "predicament. We are caught in it; it is something compulsory, urgent, dangerous, and tempting. We are surrounded by enormous, mysterious, only half-friendly forces."[16] Our numbered days are as grass and we must fight to sustain them in a world notoriously not molded after our heart's desire—not cut to the human scale, though men arise in it and have their petty peep-holes upon it. To live out our brief days is inevitably to "look before and after / And pine for what is not." In a lapsing present we must profit for an unknown future in spite of a fatal track of errors past. Our unchastened desires inevitably carve us tragic niches in the realm

of immutable truth. We develop tragedy to help us suffer
and transcend the unfathomable mystery and pathos of
our mortal lot in that tragic realm. Fulke Greville's verses
are classically apt:

> *"Oh wearisome Condition of Humanity!*
> *"Borne vnder one Law, to another bound:*
> *"Vainely begot, and yet forbidden vanity,*
> *"Created sicke, commanded to be sound:*
> *What meaneth Nature by these diuerse Lawes?*
> *Passion and Reason, selfe-diuision cause:*
> *Is it the marke, or Maiesty of Power*
> *To make offences that it may forgiue?*
> *Nature herselfe, doth her owne selfe defloure,*
> *To hate those errors she her selfe doth giue.*[17]

By giving aesthetic form and value to the chaos of our
experience, tragedy helps us to endure such truth about
ourselves as captive animals before we are transcendent
spirits. Hence it comes home to our burdened bosoms
more profoundly, more movingly, than ever comedy can;
for it would write the true and valiant record, however
sad, of our brief and troubled passage through the "unfathomable sea" of time.

And yet mere "existence is a joy to the sportive side
of our nature," as children and clowns have reminded
us. "What indeed could be more exhilarating . . . if only
we are not too exacting, and do not demand of it irrelevant
perfections? The art of life is to keep step with the celestial
orchestra that beats the measure of our career, and gives
the cue for our exits and our entrances. Why should we
willingly miss anything, or precipitate anything, or be
angry with folly, or in despair at any misadventure? In
this world there should be none but gentle tears, and
fluttering tip-toe loves. It is a great Carnival, and amongst
these lights and shadows of comedy, these roses and vices
of the playhouse, there is no abiding." In the "key" songs
of Shakespeare's comedies is there not often an attitude
toward life consonant with Santayana's wise one? Jaques

and Prospero discoursing on our playhouse world and Feste singing tenderly of its fleeting joys and sorrows to be taken in season reveal their creator en rapport with the philosopher from whom I have been freely quoting. For Shakespeare, too, knew that it is "no interruption to experience to master experience, as tragedy aspires to do; nor is it an interruption to sink into its episodes and render them consummate, which is the trick of comedy"—comedy, "the irresponsible, complete, extreme expression of each moment."[18]

By "moment" I understand that brief span of perception on the human scale in which the radical contrast between our knowledge of a thing and its conventional representation (or between that representation and another at a still farther remove from the known fact or thing) amuses consciousness, uncommitted in children or detached in adults. Adult consciousness is a house of many chambers; but in my comic "moment" we forget "time's battering ram" and look not before and after it, but at the target in all its absurdity when immediately juxtaposed to the flux of existence. The latest concepts of time in the age of relativity and the split atom do not, I think, undercut what I might, with a bow to Jaques, call "seven ages of man" time; or, with one to the common man, call "Tom, Dick, and Harry" time. Should our astronauts plunge through light years of time, mother earth will inevitably remain their home base, and home time will govern their consciousness and measure the comic incidents that, we landlubbers may hope, will relieve their journeyings. Different heads here at home take different lengths of time to get the point of a joke and some never get it; but the point always appears in that flash of consciousness that is my "moment."

I am aware that I sail over epistemological and ontological deeps. I can merely say that to me a sense of the comic seems inseparable from animal faith in a material world in physical time, perforce known to consciousness (one

of its creations) through our intuition of essences manifested by that existential flux. These signs give us working
knowledge of things that in themselves we can never
know. That subjective idealists and persistent transcen-
dentalists who mistake such signs for the things they signify are comically weak in a sense of the comic supports,
I think, my position.

"Everything in nature," then, is Janus-faced: felt on the
pulses in all its fatal implications in the realm of immutable
truth and doomed to imperfect flowering in the jungle
of existence, it shows its tragic visage; caught on the wing
by a childlike sportiveness for its pristine presence in
consciousness, oblivious of time and change, and then
seen in absurd contrast with the conventions that they
breed, it reveals its comic face.[19]

But the comic face of anything shifts if we look long
before and after that moment—to its involvement in onrushing life over time. To cohere and persist in the world,
we must moralize the spectacle, distinguish a better from
a worse in our particular predicament; things then,
chameleon-like, become now humorous, now tragic, now
satiric, now ironic in hue—terms all akin to the fundamentally comic and calling for nice differentiation from it.
Sustained existence in society forces man's adult world
(as Santayana writes) to be

> a perpetual caricature of itself; at every moment it is the mock-
> ery and the contradiction of what it is pretending to be. But
> as it nevertheless intends all the time to be something different
> and highly dignified, at the next moment it corrects and checks
> and tries to cover up the absurd thing it was; so that a conven-
> tional world, a world of masks, is superimposed on the reality,
> and passes in every sphere of human interest for the reality
> itself. Humour is the perception of this illusion, the fact al-
> lowed to pierce here and there through the convention, whilst
> the convention continues to be maintained, as if we had not
> observed its absurdity. Pure comedy is more radical, cruder,
> in a certain sense less human; because comedy throws the
> convention over altogether, revels for a moment in the fact,

and brutally says to the notions of mankind, as if it slapped them in the face, There, take that! That's what you really are! At this the polite world pretends to laugh, not tolerantly as it does at humour, but a little angrily. It does not like to see itself by chance in the glass, without having had time to compose its features for demure self-contemplation. 'What a bad mirror,' it exclaims; 'it must be concave or convex; for surely I never looked like that. Mere caricature, farce, and horseplay. Dickens[20] exaggerates; *I* never was so sentimental as that; *I* never saw anything so dreadful; *I* don't believe there were ever any people like Quilp, or Squeers, or Serjeant Buzfuz.' But the polite world is lying; there *are* such people; we are such people ourselves in our true moments, in our veritable impulses; but we are careful to stifle and to hide those moments from ourselves and from the world; to purse and pucker ourselves into the mask of our conventional personality; and so simpering, we profess that it is very coarse and inartistic of Dickens to undo our life's work for us in an instant, and remind us of what we are.... We do not consent to be absurd, though absurd we are. We have no fundamental humility. We do not wish the moments of our lives to be caught by a quick eye in their grotesque initiative, and to be pilloried in this way before our own eyes.... pure comedy is scornful, merciless, devastating, holding no door open to anything beyond. Cultivated English feeling winces at this brutality, although the common people love it in clowns and puppet shows; ... Dickens [and, one may add, Shakespeare in Falstaff on "honor," for example], who surely was tender enough, had so irresistible a comic genius that it carried him beyond the gentle humour which most Englishmen possess to the absolute grotesque reality. Squeers, for instance, when he sips the wretched dilution which he has prepared for his starved and shivering little pupils, smacks his lips and cries: 'Here's richness!' It is savage comedy; humour would come in if we understood (what Dickens does not tell us) that the little creatures were duly impressed and thought the thin liquid truly delicious. I suspect that English sensibility prefers the humour and wit of Hamlet to the pure comedy of Falstaff; and that even in Aristophanes it seeks consolation in the lyrical poetry for the flaying of human life in the comedy itself. Tastes are free; but we should not deny that in merciless and rollicking comedy life is caught in the act. The most grotesque creatures of Dickens are not exaggerations or mockeries of something other than themselves; they arise because nature generates them, like toadstools; they exist because they can't help it, as we all do. The fact that these perfectly self-justified beings are absurd appears only by comparison, and from outside; circumstances, or the expectations of other people, make them ridiculous and force them to contradict themselves; but in nature it is no crime to be exceptional. Often, but for the savagery of the average man, it would not even be a misfortune. The sleepy fat boy in *Pickwick* looks foolish; but in himself he is no more foolish, nor less solidly self-justified, than a pumpkin lying on the ground. Toots seems ridiculous; and we laugh heartily at his incoherence, his beautiful waistcoats, and his extreme modesty; but when did anybody more obviously grow into what he is because he couldn't grow otherwise? So with Mr. Pickwick, and Sam Weller, and Mrs. Gamp, and Micawber, and all the rest of this wonderful gallery; they are ridiculous only by accident, and in a context in which they never intended to appear. If Oedipus and Lear and Cleopatra do not seem ridiculous, it is only because tragic reflection has taken them out of the context in which, in real life, they would have figured.[21] If we saw them as facts, and not as emanations of a poet's dream, we should laugh at them till doomsday; what grotesque presumption, what silly whims, what mad contradiction of the simplest realities! Yet we should not laugh at them without feeling how real their griefs were; as real and terrible as the griefs of children and of dreams. But facts, however serious inwardly, are always absurd outwardly;[22] and the just critic of life sees both truths at once, as Cervantes did in *Don Quixote*. A pompous idealist who does not see the ridiculous in *all* things is the dupe of his sympathy and abstraction; and a clown, who does not see that these ridiculous creatures are living quite in earnest, is the dupe of his egotism.[23] Dickens saw the absurdity, and understood the life; I think he was a good philosopher.[24]

Shakespeare, too, was such a "good philosopher." He "saw the absurdity and understood the life" supremely well—especially in his maturest comedies where his rendering of character in action is pervaded by embracive humor, moving and amusing and pathetic and comic.[25]

The sustained quotations from Santayana will reverberate, I think, as we advance. For the moment, we note that humor, as he discerningly explicates it, maintains the conventions that ongoing life inevitably imposes, the while it is acutely aware of their absurdity beside the flux of animal facts beneath them.[26] The radically comic, however, "scornful, merciless, devastating, holding no door open to anything beyond," roughly brushes aside those absurd social conventions to expose baldly the facts and revel for a free moment in their blunt contrast with those pretenses behind which they hide.

Some dramatists today, understandably full of despair or satiric disgust before the terrible miscarriages of reason in our century, often leave us with a feeling of the hopeless absurdity of human life, if too rarely with a sense of its traditional tragic stature. If life "is free play fundamentally and would like to be free play altogether,"[27] as Santayana and Shakespeare in his "festive"[28] comedies remind us, it has trouble appearing so to heirs of Buchenwald and Hiroshima. To Ionesco the "human drama is as absurd as it is painful. It all comes to the same thing, anyway; comic and tragic are merely two aspects of the same situation. . . . There are no alternatives; if man is not tragic, he is ridiculous and painful, 'comic' in fact, and by revealing his absurdity one can achieve a sort of tragedy."[29] Comedy for Ionesco and some other moderns achieves a "sort of tragedy" by ceasing to turn freely on one pole of the comic—the play instinct that vents itself in free laughter in the "irresponsible, complete, and extreme expression of each moment." Ionesco calls *The Chairs* a "tragic farce."[30] But Shakespeare's "festive" comedies can be twisted into no such genre. Jan Kott sidesteps or distorts them in reducing Shakespeare to our existentialistic "contemporary."[31] And when Brecht finds "horror in the heart of farce" he is considering it more curiously than does the common man who (with Shakespeare) drinks his farce neat in the moment.[32]

Now in the truly mature man with a sense of humor, a taste for what I shall call the radically comic demands "fundamental humility"; for in a way it is amoral and infra-human. He accepts the relativity of the existent with respect to the infinite. His point of vantage is enough aside from the hurly-burly to behold all the forms and conventions of life as but one casting from infinity upon this bank and shoal of time. For him, life's fitful fever is, after all (comically to mix Macbeth's metaphor), but a teapot tempest. By laughing at the absurdity of the spectacle he gains freedom from the "heavy and the weary weight of all this unintelligible world." In such quick and humble laughter before the immediate as it intrinsically is, absurd when apprehended outwardly in contrast with the infinite storehouse of what might conceivably have existed had God so willed it, a man is, surely, more spiritual than when he egotistically protests existence and follows his blind will. Of course I mean the instantaneously existent in its primordial innocence before it collides with everything else in scrambling after its little day in the sun, before its involvement in an onrushing world where wills inevitably clash, "month follow[s] month with woe, and year wake[s] year to sorrow."[33] "When laughter is humble, when it is not based on self-esteem, it is wiser than tears."[34] Have not sages and saints in their "fundamental humility" seen this intrinsic innocence in creation from instant to instant prior to what man makes of man or time of life and, becoming again not unlike little children, echoed their happy laughter before the absurdity of all forms that enfold the immediate and contrast with it? For more than a thousand years the strains of oriental wisdom in Christianity disciplined the egocentric spirit of western man to this "fundamental humility," basic if a mature man is to catch the radically comic aspect of all things. Such wisdom underlies medieval praise of folly and the fool.[35] One suspects that the radically comic was no stranger to joyous Saint Francis, however much he was a man acquainted with grief. Everyone knows what praise wise Erasmus gave folly and that his sainted friend Sir Thomas More jested with his executioner when, "goinge vppe the scaffold, which was so weake that it was ready to fall, he saide merilye to Master Lieutenaunte: 'I pray you, Master Lieutenaunte, see me salf vppe, and for my cominge downe let me shifte for my self.' ''[36] Lincoln kept one eye cocked for the comic, if behind scenes a man of sorrows. The quick sense for the comic among the Irish is inseparable from the ability of a volatile, mercurial people, never too heavily saddled with this world's goods, to live irresponsibly in the moment and laugh at all onerous duties and commitments. And surely the wonderfully swift sense of it among American Negroes is inseparable from their long enforced humility and concomitant animal relaxation before the bald facts. Often the poor and the dispossessed with little to lose or gain in this world join hands with men disillusioned with the world in perceiving the fundamentally comic nature of all its vanities. Where children are uncommitted (they think), such folk are detached; hence all can laugh alike at the radically comic. That mature man who enjoys it has perforce known humor too—has a measure of sufferance and acceptance within his amusement before the absurd spectacle of the existent. Laughter may not make men gods as Voltaire declared it does, but it is akin to divine philosophy. Democritus laughed at the dancing atoms. If man were truly humble before his current conquest of the atomic dance, we could not cry of his way with atoms:

> But man, proud man,
> Drest in a little brief authority,
> Most ignorant of what he's most assur'd
> (His glassy essence), like an angry ape,
> Plays such fantastic tricks before high heaven
> As make the angels weep.[37]

Theoretically, *any* fact in momentary contrast with its encrusting convention is comic if playfully beheld with detachment. But civilized men are too deeply committed to their precious "conventions" of human decency to see anything but ineffable horror in the crimes of men in our terrible century who would shame Swift's Yahoos. They only could laugh at Belsen and Buchenwald. Perhaps the most horrible aspect of Hitler and his henchmen was their total lack of humane humor, of any "fundamental humility," its base. If we are amused in a fashion by Chaplin's "The Great Dictator" and Brecht's *Arturo Ui*, it is only after art has distanced the brute facts behind them.[38]

Humor like Charles Lamb's tempers a taste for the radically comic with wit and wisdom—with sustained sufferance of the absurd convention. Sufferance is a better term, perhaps, than tolerance, for humor, as I noted, is not necessarily genial, as the second term might imply. Those little victims of Squeers in *Nicholas Nickleby* do not emerge as humorous figures because they do not appear "duly impressed" by that villain's pretense that his "wretched dilution" is "truly delicious." They do not appear as accepting the absurd pretense, and if they did, the humor would not be genial because they could hardly be thought pleased by that pretense. Humor perforce scorns not even the radically comic's way with conventions, for it knows itself tethered to the comic moment in time's transshifting. We tend to trust a man with a sense of humor because we instinctively feel that he will, the while he perceives the absurdity of the conventional, not protest it over hotly since he knows the inevitability of conventions of some sort in a continuing world where millions of men must somehow keep heads above water in the rough sea of social life. Humor, unlike the radically comic, has looked before and after to discover that all of us are "ridiculous only by accident, in a context in which we never intended to appear." Of the most absurd among us, it declares, "God made him, and therefore let him pass for a man." Its well-known playfulness is perhaps a transmutation of the animal sportiveness of the child.[39] Its covertness and indirectness in technique[40] spring from its quiet awareness of the animal or existential fact beneath the conventional mask, yet its sufferance of both. And so it naturally has an affinity for wit and paradox and ambiguity and word play of all sorts, for irony and burlesque—all terms to be reckoned with.

Yet, however ultimate the civilizing force of humor in a mature man, the radically comic itself—"scornful, merciless, devastating, holding no door open to anything beyond"—is forever a healthful check upon creatures given to pride of life in Vanity Fair, for it humbles them utterly in stripping them bare of all their worldly garb. If children and clowns need it less they love it more because, essentially impervious to humor, they either know lightly or ignore the welter of conventions, inseparable from social life over long time, that humor is forever aware of. The radically comic is, as I have said, intrinsically amoral in focusing directly on the object or fact and heeding not its involvement in a vast spread of life—in our tangled web of "mingled yarn, good and ill together." Now this radically comic moment yields not alone to humor, which more or less genially suffers conventions because it is too aware of the relativity of things to moralize the spectacle vehemently. It yields in time just as readily to judgment that does variously moralize the absurd spectacle. The first fruit is then what I shall call the critically or correctively comic—clay for molding critical comedies as different as the plays of Aristophanes, Jonson, Molière, Goldsmith, Shaw, and Ionesco. Being and becoming or essence and existence are the warp and woof of life, forever in flux. Caught in it, men as social beings long ago discovered that the momentary laughter of the simply comic can be sustained or repeated enough either to needle or to club us into conduct that hugs the healthy facts more than it tends to do in the cross-currents of this crooked world. To ridicule folly is often to shame it into sense, man being an egotistic animal eager for the esteem of his fellows and shy of their critical laughter that would spotlight his absurdities.[41] But when judgment so moralizing the absurd spectacle proceeds with ire and indignation heaped on the heads of men to make them mend their ways—to rebuke what reason and morality deem folly and vice—it shades into the satiric.

"The spectrum-analysis of satire runs from the red of invective at one end to the violet of the most delicate irony at the other. Beyond either end of the scale, literature runs off into forms that are not perceptible as satire. The ultra-violet is pure criticism; the infra-red is direct reproof or abuse, untransformed by art."[42] The truly satiric, according to a host of witnesses from Roman days to our own, involves angry laughter, not laughter at the mere ridiculousness of things. Hate animates it in the classical masters from Juvenal to Swift—hate that would, with distortion of materials for emphasis, rebuke and reform vice and folly by holding them up to scorn and derision for expulsion or reformation. A seemingly cool detachment must hold in leash its indignation when at white heat; and it has, of course, manifold gradations of intensity when modified by comic ingredients, as Horace and Goldsmith, contrasted with Juvenal and Swift, instantly remind us.[43] Nor have its greatest successes been in the dramatic form, as these names also remind us; for the satiric precludes that sympathetic identification with his various characters that a successful dramatist must have. Furthermore, in a comedy the satiric, the humorous, and the comic (radical and/or critical) may each mix swiftly with the others in, apparently, as many minglings as there are experiences of life and expressions of it in art forms. Hence the baffling divergencies that arise in understanding the terms as we juggle them in literary criticism. Underlying attitude as mobile as life determines what one tone—comic, humorous, satiric, ironic, and so on—is to dominate at any one point in any given work of art. Both the radically comic and the satiric brusquely and scornfully expose the bald actualities, the latter ramifying over time and moralizing with varying degrees of ire and indignation the clash between the social pretense and the animal fact. The humorous, conscious over time of the facts behind the pretenses, more or less genially maintains the conventions, being kept from the rigid moralization of satire by a profound sense of the relativity of all things and by a playful spirit, the latter present in the radically comic, but neither present in the satiric. The critically comic, the humorous, and the satiric all involve a sustained framework of conventional social life spread over time; but the radically comic, it will be remembered, is in essence "the irresponsible, complete, extreme expression of each moment." The radically comic—"scornful, merciless, devastating, holding no door open to anything beyond"—swiftly spawns the critically comic as time spreads around the moment and breeds moral life. And this critically comic as easily slips into the satiric (witness Ben Jonson's comedies) as time lengthens and as scorn and derision, ire and indignation, rebuke the pretenses that seem insufferably over time to falsify the healthy animal facts. Massinger's *A New Way to Pay Old Debts* will remind any reader how an overt moralizing intent can stifle the genuinely comic—move it toward the satiric and the tragic—even as Middleton's *A Trick to Catch the Old One* will remind him how an aloof detachment in the playwright can free the truly comic spirit. The radically comic is intrinsically a thing of the moment; the critically comic looks beyond that moment to its moral involvement; so too does the humorous, but with a pervasive sense of relativity and with a spirit of playfulness that is forward in the radically comic but recessive in the critically comic; the satiric, involving time and morality, sacrifices both that sense of relativity and of play. In the humorous the ego is muted; in the satiric it is strident. We may well recall what we early learned: Shakespeare's comedy is not often vigorously critical (though much formal comedy is) and even less often satirical. The sufferance of convention, the sense of relativity, and the playfulness of humor constantly check in Shakespeare any sustained critical intent and satiric bite and sting for reformation—although his cornerstones and timbers are often the radically comic. Furthermore, his comedy is profoundly modified by poetry and romance, by music and dance. To his fellow Ben Jonson one looks for critical comedy with strong satiric strains in the classical tradition.[44]

Before we explore Shakespeare's course with the comic and its kin, clarification of still other terms that run with the comic is in order—comic though one may himself inevitably appear in trying to pin down terms that are almost as free-footed as the life on the wing that they try to net. Because the comic forever has its right foot in the flux of things, its object at any one juncture slips that net even as it is captured.

The ironic is a difficult domain, yet unavoidable in any scrutiny of the comic. If the comic is grounded in the absurd contrast between actual fact and its conventional representation, taken playfully within the given moment, irony is the "flash given off when two contradictory absolutes collide."[45] The ironic bows to the impact of the actual facts in collision, but does so, not like the purely comic in amoral, "irresponsible, complete, extreme expression of each moment," but so as to stress the conflict, clash, or tension between actualities, whatever the absurd comic gap between them and their appearances. For David Worcester irony "is a form of criticism, and all irony is satirical, though not all satire is ironical."[46] For him the

elements of general satire ... [are] invective, burlesque, and irony. Irony in its own right has expanded from a minute verbal phenomenon to a philosophy, a way of facing the cosmos. ... We begin with verbal irony; we end with cosmic irony. Between these terminal stages, we may mark two convenient milestones. Irony of manner betokens a deliberate pose on our author's part, a manipulation of the literary personality. Just as the principles of burlesque are extensions of the principles of invective, so an additional turn of the screw converts burlesque into Socratic or Chaucerian irony. Irony of fact, or dramatic irony, needs no ironic style or pose to make itself felt. It arises from the author's choice of subject-matter; or, more accurately, it appeals to the reader to produce the ironic lightning-flash, without help from the author.[47]

Dramatic irony involves "that sense of contradiction felt by spectators of a drama who see a character acting in ignorance of his condition."[48] Two or more actualities are at irreconcilable odds, unbeknownst to one or more participants in the situation, but usually known to at least one of them. And those irreconcilable actualities fall within the compass of the truth. Dramatic irony strictly understood appears within a complex art form that refracts a segment of life stretched over time and conveyed to an audience by physical media. Hence it is not to be divorced from the full moral and ethical dimension of life. We should never perceive what we call the irony of things were we not first moral beings caught over time among them. Irony is for adults only; children know it not at all; common clowns illustrate it but superficially. Later I shall attend to cosmic irony and mark how dramatic irony or "irony of fact and cosmic irony produce satire of a tragic cast."[49] Whereas the satiric is active, assertive, and censorious, the ironic is passive, static, and contemplative. Taken playfully in a comic milieu, irony is comic irony.

"Wit" is a tricky monosyllable that, not unlike "sin," has meant many things to many men. But its shifting senses from Renaissance and neoclassical times in England on to those of Freud and his fellows concern us less than its nature as a favorite tool of the comic in my discussion of it.[50] Wit is certainly no part of the comic as the child or the simple clown apprehends it. I would understand wit as a late sophistication in words, the chief medium of playhouse drama beyond basic miming. Wit arises long after childhood perception of the fundamentally comic has played palimpsest for "time, the mother of many mutations" (in Sidney's phrase).[51] It comes after the humorous and the satiric and the tragic have risen above our battle against the slings and arrows of outrageous fortune to which our mortal coil is heir. Wit springs from our dire need to identify with maximum precision specific objects amid the vast profusion of unplumbed things that assault our attention as we struggle among them. It depends, if we trust Santayana, upon transformation and substitution of ideas. "It has been said to consist in quick association by similarity. The substitution here must be valid, however, and the similarity real, though unforeseen. Unexpected justness makes wit. . . . It is characteristic of wit to penetrate into hidden depths of things, to pick out there some telling circumstance or relation, by noting which the whole object appears in a new and clearer light." Santayana continues: "Wit often seems malicious because analysis in discovering common traits and universal principles assimilates things at the poles of being; it can apply to cookery the formulas of theology, and find in the human heart a case of the fulcrum and lever." But all "that can be changed by the exercise of intelligence is our sense of the unity and homogeneity of the world. . . . For this reason the malicious or destructive character of intelligence must not be regarded as fundamental. Wit belittles one thing and dignifies another; and its comparisons are as often flattering as ironical." Yet wit can "condense and abstract too much. Reality is more fluid and elusive than reason, and has, as it were, more dimensions than are known even to the latest geometry. Hence the understanding, when not suffused with some glow of sympathetic emotion or some touch of mysticism, gives but a dry, crude image of the world. The quality of wit inspires more admiration than confidence. It is a merit we should miss little in any one we love." We may note that wit in Shakespeare is almost constantly so "suffused." "The same principle, however, can have more sentimental embodiments. When our substitutions are brought on by the excitement of generous emotion, we call wit inspiration. There is the same finding of new analogies, and likening of disparate things; there is the same transformation of our apperception."[52] Here the prospect unfolds upon Shakespeare's incomparably rich metaphorical statement that gives to us a unique sense of "the unity and homogeneity of the world."

The affinity of wit for the essentially comic is obvious: wit aims to disclose the "whole object . . . in a new and clearer light" through unexpected yet happy association with another object truly similar in some unforeseen way; and the purely comic, as we have seen, points abruptly within the immediate moment to the "whole object" behind its conventional mask—and ridiculously at odds with it. Hence the maturely comic inevitably finds a favorite tool in wit of all gradations.

And they are legion. I linger a moment with the so-called "lowest form of wit," the much berated pun that in the Elizabethan drama repeatedly offends good taste—or at least much modern taste. Often berated in spite of Shakespeare's love of it, Lamb's defense of it, and everyman's fun with it, the pun, riding a new tide in taste, has lately had fresh study and exaltation as a potent literary instrument.[53] What one might designate a legitimate pun does what James Joyce, William Empson, and many others have of late found it doing: by way of words identical or nearly so in sound it suddenly suspends before the mind's eye some relevant congruity in seemingly disparate objects, for the quick illumination of both. In effecting a maximum of revelation with a minimum of sound, a legitimate pun is respectful of our mature minds as they welcome as much light from as little motion and heat as may be. But an invalid or illegitimate pun—everyman's pun, so to say—subverts the aim of true wit by making a spurious substitution of a word similar or identical in sound but essentially irrelevant in sense to that which names the object for which the substitution is intended.

The adult mind, enmeshed in the mazes of conventional life, is momentarily amused by the unexpected disclosure of intrinsic *dis*similarities in things through sounds that are deceptively alike for representing them. Charles Lamb, always in an easy chair before anything comic, loved these illegitimate children of wit and defended the worst puns as the best if "by worst be only meant the most far-fetched and startling."[54] The violent contrast between verbal likenesses and factual differences does indeed relax and titillate the mind for an instant. But the substitution miscarries in deflecting attention to an arbitrary and accidental resemblance between mere words that are but breath and the total incongruity of the things they name, in frustrating expected illumination as legitimate punning does not. The illegitimate or "good" Lamb pun that merely amuses for an instant is a verbal version of the radically comic, so to say, being to wit somewhat as the farcical is to the adultly comic—a surface business altogether. If we laugh at such a pun we laugh at an accidental resemblance in two verbal conventions belied by the objects they name and unrevealing of their true footings in time and space. The genuinely witty shoots at the fact behind the fiction; the common pun leaves the fact undisclosed in exposing no more than the insignificance of similar signs for dissimilar things. Worst of all, perhaps, your punster seldom knows when to call a halt to such incidental refreshment from pointlessly accidental resemblances among words —word farce, we might call it. Yet in fairness to the weakest and most persistent of his tribe we should remember that, though bores may perpetrate puns, dullards do not.

Indescribably more satisfying than any pun *per se* is happy metaphor. One may, of course, regard it as an area of wit and inclusive of the valid pun whereby some of the congruity in objects is economically designated by words more or less alike in sound. Metaphor, as I shall understand it, in whatever form (such as the legitimate pun, simile, or personification) flashes before the full man

—"feeling mind" and "thinking heart"—unlooked for resemblances between objects that their names (differing except in valid puns) never disclose in the business of daily life. Hence metaphor, unlike the miscarrying pun, instantly satisfies adult consciousness, acutely aware of the multifariousness of phenomena, in its profound longing for unity and harmony within the labyrinth of diverse things through which over time it must thread its way. We may with Freud hold that this longing springs from a survival of a dumb sense of the unity of life known in the womb and that it is destined for full quiescence only in death; yet we hardly invalidate the fact of its presence at the heart of life, which lusts after variety within uniformity, the while reason seeks a harmony of all. The sensuous, non-intellectual, and differentiating content of metaphor, which is antecedent to wit (as I have restricted the term) on the linguistic level, is dominant, for example, when Ophelia thinks Hamlet's "noble and most sovereign reason, / Like sweet bells jangled, out of tune and harsh." When she calls Prince Hamlet before he is "blasted with ecstasy" (as she thinks) "th' expectancy and rose of the fair state . . . quite, quite down" (III.i.160–162), he is revealed to us as its finest flowering by a momentary identification of the topmost flower of the social order with that flower of the soil that for ages has best suggested the beauty of all its sweet blossoming. To take an example from Shakespearean comedy: when Rosalind suddenly likens the amorous refrains of Silvius and Phebe and Orlando and herself to the "howling of Irish wolves against the moon" (V. ii. 119), she topples the tower of love prattle to the animal base all have forgotten. Such revealing metaphor, cast in musical measures, is Apollo's first gift to a poet—that which stirs his audience to its most profound pleasure. And the metaphor in measures satisfies intrinsically, the physiologist and psychologist might remind us, largely because rhythm is vital in man's mortal life, manifested in action as diverse as our pulse beat and the tides in our affairs. They might point out, too, that such awareness of congruity within apparent diversity gratifies the healthy organism's instinct for the known and the secure even as the philosopher might add that it satisfies the soul's love of oneness and harmony amid apparent chaos. Metaphor contrasts with irony, which discloses clashing actualities of the truth and breeds tension. The pervasiveness of metaphor in the romantic comedies modifies the comic in its exposure of incongruities; through it a sense of the homogeneity of the world comes home to us.

Wit and metaphor the comic dramatist calls often to his aid as he amuses his audience by making it aware of facts behind fictions; hence my facing of notoriously complex terms from the angle of their immediate kinship with the comic as I conceive it.

I have now sought working differentiations of some familiar but elusive terms that are basic for the impending scrutiny of Shakespeare and the comic: the comic (radical and corrective) and the humorous, the satiric and the ironic, and wit and metaphor. And I have glanced at the realm of the tragic; time enough to probe it (and the pathetic) when we encounter them interwoven with the comic and its kindred in the plays. This summary view of the elusively familiar will need much focusing as I face great exemplars of a complex art form wherein the comic and its many allies have a stature at once less and larger than in workaday life—playhouse drama in Shakespeare's day.

Perhaps I should rehearse "some platitudes concerning drama" if I am to set fairly the props of my stage for passing views of comic strains in a complex art form. Although the form of comedy is not my primary interest, my reader is entitled to know just how I shall be construing some of the old and familiar terms of dramatic criticism that I inevitably use.

Criticism in our time has brought a quickened appreciation of the role of imagery in Shakespearean drama for delineating character; for evoking mood, tone, atmosphere, and setting; for illustrating theme; and even for integrating design. Symbolic meaning, ritual patterning, and mythological undertones have, too, justly drawn attention, sometimes forgetful of the exigencies of playhouse drama in Elizabethan days. But iterative imagery and these other elements have not been such basically structural ones in traditional drama for a popular audience as plot, however shifted its role from Sophocles to Beckett. At the risk of appearing as antiquated as Aristotle to avant-gardists, I shall use the term to designate the artistically organized record of the impacts that active individuals in a group make on one another in the simulation of a segment of life, projected in mime and dialogue by actors and other physical media to entertain an audience, at once individual and composite, in a popular theater. By curiosity, suspense, and surprise, your dramatist so manipulates those impacts as to arouse in that audience emotional tension that mounts upward through struggle, conflict, and crisis to climax and resolution. The medium (after mime) is primarily verbal images in prose or verse (or both) spoken by actors on a stage and supported by physical media as various as costumes, settings, music, and the dance. Involved, too, are many age-old conventions peculiar to the form and subserving its ends. At once your dramatist must simultaneously evoke interest and impart knowledge of relevant antecedent action in terms of onstage situation and character, for he has perforce plunged *in medias res.* When we look behind scenes and acts into basic design, we see that a play inevitably develops in three movements or parts of varying length and weight. Slipping into Johnsonese, one may speak of explication of situation, followed by complication of situation, and that capped by resolution of complication. (Students will of course recall classic terms behind mine: protasis, epitasis, and catastrophe; and Aristotle's exordium, complication, and denouement or catastrophe.) All must be funneled through dialogue that seems lifelike, but is something more and something less in being at once the vehicle for projecting action, developing characters, and, to a great degree, creating setting, mood, and tone, and sustaining theme, and suggesting any symbolic meaning—all such stage traffic for Shakespeare (if not always for O'Neill) usually being cast within the narrow confines of two or three hours. Inevitably devices and conventions arise in drama to effect so much in such quick order. Central, perhaps, is contrast—vivid contrast that is emotionally stimulating and rapid in revelation. And, as we have seen, contrast to evoke laughter is at the heart of the comic.[55]

Now if a dramatist, aiming to simulate a segment of life, excerpts from it the predominantly tragic aspects (as I have suggested them) in a span of experience, real or imaginary, to compose his plot and portray his agents, and so treats them as to stress their disastrous involvement in time and space by their unenlightened will and desire in order that his audience may somehow find a surcease from pity and fear in their own lives through seeing the like writ large in the misfortunes of their fellowmen on the stage—he writes what we call tragedy. If, on the other hand, he excerpts primarily comic aspects (as I have explicated them) to compose his plot and portray his agents, and so treats them as to keep chiefly to their surface contacts with life that his audience may laugh or smile in happy release from care and (usually) feel the social correction of laughter—he writes comedy. Of course tone and intent in both tragedy and comedy vary a thousand ways as the tragic and the comic, the humorous, the satiric, the ironic, and so on are crisscrossed, and various devices, rhetorical and mechanical, are employed to shift mood and atmosphere. Both kinds of drama use the same basic mediums, throw different aspects of the same human predicament into different perspectives, and vary somewhat in their forms, techniques, and expression.

Perhaps my observations on the nature of the comic and its kin should for a moment confront representative concepts of comedy in Shakespeare's day.[56] Even as it is today, comedy then was such a capacious term that it often meant little more than a motley play that "beginneth sorrowfully, and endeth merrily, contrary to a tragedy."[57] In the usual stage comedy fun and foolishness mingled with more or less serious business until every Jack somehow got his Jill at the finish. The familiar complaint made by Sidney as a traditionalist that "all their Playes bee neither right Tragedies, nor right Comedies, mingling Kinges and Clownes,"[58] heard on the eve of Shakespeare's career, strikes at the long-time illicit love of the genres for each other, particularly in England. Mighty Ben Jonson went his own individual way in making "right comedies" and spoke out vigorously in definition of comedy as critical and satirical. But perhaps there is no more valid voice describing the run of playhouse comedies than that of prolific Thomas Heywood, heard in 1612 just at the finish of Shakespeare's career:

[A comedy] is pleasantly contriued with merry accidents, and intermixt with apt and witty iests, to present before the Prince at certain times of solemnity, or else merily fitted to the stage. And what is then the subiect of this harmelesse mirth? either in the shape of a Clowne, to shew others their slouenly and vnhansome behauiour, that they may reforme that simplicity in themselues, which others make their sport, lest they happen to become the like subiect of generall scorne to an auditory, else it intreates of loue, deriding foolish inamorates, who spend their ages, their spirits, nay themselues, in the seruile and ridiculous imployments of their Mistresses: and these are mingled with sportfull accidents, to recreate such as of themselues are wholly deuoted to Melancholly, which corrupts the bloud: or to refresh such weary spirits as are tired with labour, or study, to moderate the cares and heauinesse of the minde, that they may returne to their trades and faculties with more zeale and earnestnesse, after some small soft and pleasant retirement.[59]

This definition, from no closet theorist but a popular playwright who produced plays by the hundreds, embraces the essentials of the comic as I have tried to explicate them. Primarily a comedy is "pleasantly contriued with merry accidents, and intermixt with apt and witty iests." It is "merily fitted to the stage." Its "harmelesse mirth" either uses "a Clowne, to shew others their slouenly and vnhansome behauiour" with the intent of mending their "simplicity" lest they become the butt of sport and "generall scorne" like the enacted characters; or else it derides the foolishness of lovers to breed better sense in them. Mingled with such critically comic strains are merely "sportfull accidents" to "recreate" the melancholy and free the weary of spirit from care "that they may returne to their trades and faculties with more zeale and earnestnesse, after some small soft and pleasant retirement." In Heywood's conception of the comic, the playful or sportive spirit weaves loosely with the critical or didactic in a recipe broad enough to embrace comedy as bent on correction as Jonson's and as unbent on correction as Shakespeare's.[60] I shall recur to this central statement by Heywood as I seek to trace Shakespeare's way with the comic.[61]

A preliminary word about some stock tools of the comic in the formal comedies is perhaps in order. Some such devices and conventions have roots "lost in the dark backward and abysm of folk-custom."[62] Anyone looking at man in society over long time observes that the comic aspects of his seven ages are marked by much iteration as basic animal impulses persist in individuals beneath the skin of civilized society, meet similar checks or channelings, and hence invite treatment by comic art in stock or stereotyped forms and figures. The comic operates, as I have insisted, in the free play and amusing clash between such forms and conventions and the real facts—incongruity is a dominant word in the criticism of comedy.

Hence the type characters in comedy from ancient days down. Hence the gull, the parasite, the *miles gloriosus,* the witty slave, the outwitted father, and so on in Latin comedy. Hence the various masks of *commedia dell'arte* and the comic devil and the Vice of the old moralities. And to focus and exploit for comedy the many stock postures that life imposes upon us, the various fools, buffoons, and jesters that flourished over medieval times and have their descendants today in cartoons and comic strips and in the latest comedy hits on Broadway. The shrewish wife and the henpecked husband, for example, are accretions from innumerable checks and counter-checks between the factual female of the species and the egotistical male. Chaunticleer and Pertelote are delicious barnyard parodies of this eternal tug-of-war within the marriage bond, and the Wife of Bath a supremely comic Penthesilea in the battle for "maiestrie" by the woman. Petruchio is the dominant rooster turning the tables—he thinks. All such figures and many others incarnate abiding comic aspects of our common humanity that the comic artist projects either to amuse or to correct us or to do both. From classical antiquity and the Middle Ages, the Renaissance inherited a rich store of such tools, devices, and techniques that have been described in many books. I can touch only the surface of some salient ones as they appear and reappear in the plays of Shakespeare.

CHAPTER II

The RADICALLY COMIC DOMINANT:
The Comedy of Errors, The Taming of the Shrew, and *The Merry Wives of Windsor*

What I have defined as the radically comic is, essentially, the farcical. The purely farcical appears when a given event or situation contrasts abruptly and absurdly in the moment with the normal and the expected as custom and convention will have it, and attention radiates not at all over emotional ties in time and space. Hence it excludes characterization in depth; for what is character but an individual man's compounding of the comic, the tragic, and all their kin over long time? We meet the purely farcical in practical jokes, in the antics of clowns, in the slapstick of vaudeville, in Punch and Judy puppets and all their tribe. When such wooden dolls are jerked through absurd situations, sympathy, that mortal foe of the farcical, is nil. The Petrouchka who evokes our sympathy and pity is a complex fellow who does not belie my generalization: a dancer enacts a puppet that symbolizes man's tragic predicament; and his farcical puppet stature breeds involved ironic tension between petty symbol and great things signified.

I pause for a moment with formal farce before trailing the farcical in comedies in which it is dominant, conscious always of the ingredients that may combine with it: the critically comic, the humorous, the satiric, the witty, the ironic, the tragic, the romantic and the poetic, and music and dance. Our eyes will range over the structures of the comedies, but focus on the stones of the comic with which they are built.

Farce stems out of elemental religious ceremonials in ancient Greece and Rome, has a vigorous life there, a complex history over medieval times in folk and religious areas, and, quickened anew by associations with its Latin ancestors, flowers out in Italy during Shakespeare's days both in *commedia dell'arte* and *commedia erudita*. In such Italian drama

> it is not always easy to distinguish between comedy and farce, for the dramatis personae are constant and the material is common to both grades of entertainment. The type of interest evoked may be taken as a touchstone. When a play interests us because of the fortunes of certain characters it appeals to our affections and may be called romantic comedy. When it interests to see how a given end is to be achieved, how a wager is to be lost or won, how a slave is to be smuggled in, its appeal is intellectual and belongs to the comedy of intrigue; when we care for neither characters nor motives, but are content to be amused by whatever absurdity may be trumped up, it is farce. We do not care about Pantalone and his mistress; we do not mind if Colombina and Pulcinella quarrel for ever; nor do we ask for probability in the ways that they obtain or cheat each other; all that we want is to see them doing it again; to watch them fight on the merest excuse, to run into their own booby traps. We want a palpable gross play. On such licence the Commedia dell'arte throve.[1]

Such farce is obviously a dramatic construction from what I have called the radically comic; and comedy of intrigue that Miss Lea describes is its brother in making no appeal to our emotions.

My interest is now Shakespeare's way with the farcical in three plays written in the fore part of his career: *The Comedy of Errors* (1592 or 1593), *The Taming of the Shrew* (1594–1598), and *The Merry Wives of Windsor* (1600). All are commonly called farces; yet each has a significant infusion of other stuff to which I shall give attention later. In traditional farce, events are uppermost; hence, wearing blinkers for the moment, I focus on them in these three plays.

If the first of these plays be not the first comedy that Shakespeare wrote—and good argument makes it that—it is certainly the one that should first arrest us, for no other of his plays gives the merely farcical such sustained illustration. It shows Shakespeare at the outset building comedy on the bedrock comic—the radically comic as I have described it. The farcical was dominant in Shakespeare's immediate comic heritage in the drama; *The Second Shepherd's Play, Gammer Gurton's Needle*, and many interludes, come at once to mind—as do Plautus and Terence. *The Comedy of Errors* derives in part from the *Menaechmi* of Plautus, which deals with the adventures and mishaps of indistinguishable twin brothers, and in part from the duplication of twins (twin servants for twin masters), which Shakespeare found in Plautus's *Amphitruo*. This doubling of twins quadruples occasions for amusing incidents pitched upon accident—makes comic confusion more absurdly confounded. Mistaken identity and disguise are staples in comedy from the beginning. The reason is obvious: What could be more radically comic than quick contrasts between disguises, particularly the "disguise" of twins, that cover different entities with which in the extant moment they are absurdly at odds? The absurd jams that the pairs of twins inevitably breed, laughably clashing with primary facts, give the play its vigorously farcical base. All such comic effects turn upon the ridiculous clash between actuality and appearance in the moment when it is shorn of complications of character bred by time and space. Shakespeare dexterously juggles the two sets of twins and their confused associates into one comic posture after another. The fun mounts as absurd situation piles upon absurd situation with an almost mathematical progression into the last scene. That little masterpiece of construction resolves all; even the courtesan gets her diamond.[2] And all is "pleasant contrivance" of "merry incidents" for "harmless mirth," "sportfull accidents" to "recreate" and "refresh" us with no intent to correct or reform anybody. Yet into this warp of the farcical is woven a certain woof of the romantic—even of the potentially tragic. Such secondary threads I shall glance at later. The dominant warp is radically comic in the way facts or events always are when faced foursquarely and apart from their moral involvement in time and space. Such farcical movement that looks to events of the moment in all their existential absurdity appeals to the instinct for free play in an audience that keeps as its childhood inheritance a delight in the irrationally funny.

With its jolly tumbling movement, the doggerel used by the Dromios and others in the farcical dialogue introduces a tempo and rhythm at odds with any mighty lines in our minds or with normally poised ones in areas of the play that are something other than farcical. Such movement tickles our sense of the hurly-burly of events in which the radically comic lives, and happily sustains them as they mesh together into the farcical action of the play.[3] As the beatings of the Dromios attest the roughly farcical quality of the action, so their punning may remind us that the frame of identical twins doubled is itself a double pun-like device—radical divergencies in objects misleadingly, but amusingly, concealed behind identical names or appearances, with little plumbing of the individual idiosyncrasies of those objects.

With this farcical fabric of *The Comedy of Errors* in mind —many funny mix-ups bred by pairs of identical twins as the actualities of their diverse persons clash momentarily with the accidents of their similar appearances—I turn to *The Taming of the Shrew*. Some students hold that Shakespeare reworked an old anonymous play, *The Taming of a Shrew* (printed in 1594), which combined the taming story, the wooing of the shrew's younger sister (from

George Gascoigne's *Supposes*, acted in 1566 and printed in 1573, and a translation of Ariosto's *I Suppositi* of 1509), and the hoaxing of Christopher Sly. Other students (more recently) argue that *A Shrew* is a bad quarto of *The Shrew*. Certainly *The Shrew* effects a better combination of stories than *A Shrew* does.

To consider first what first we face in *The Shrew*— Christopher Sly. A sustained figure in the old play who emerges comically at the right places, Sly is dropped in *The Shrew* after his effective use in the Induction—nobody knows just why. Some say that an epilogue featuring him has been lost; some, that Sly came to be omitted in performance because anticlimactic after the liveliness of the shrew-taming episodes; and some, that the comedians were expected to sustain Sly by improvisation throughout the play. Because *The Shrew* lacks both an epilogue and the incidental comments that in *A Shrew* Sly makes upon the taming he is witnessing, some hold that such comments and any epilogue were deliberately omitted as inartistic interruptions.[4] If Sly, drunk and somnolent, was simply dragged off the stage as the taming game and love intrigue got under way, perhaps the Elizabethan audience, absorbed by such lively doings, hardly missed him. We see Sly thrown at once into a highly farcical posture and drawn with verve and vigor. Catapulting a tipsy tinker into the luxurious setting of a grand gentleman and fooling him into thinking he is metamorphosed into just that creates a radically comic situation. Tipsiness is an age-old instrument of the radically comic because drink is a welcome remover of illusions or a notorious breeder of wild ones; it will arrest us when we meet those great bibblers Sir Toby Belch and Sir John Falstaff. Sly is saturated enough with the illusion that he has indeed become a fine gentleman; we relish the contrast between the fact and his delusion. We may reflect that he will need Petruchio's lesson in shrew-taming when he sobers up back home with his own shrew, now no doubt "nursing her

wrath to keep it warm" for her Tam's return.⁵ Tossing
Sly out in *A Shrew* at its finish caps the practical joke
played on him.

By way of the joke on Sly, we move adroitly into the
play proper. Its two farcical strains are dovetailed together
with far greater skill than they are in Shakespeare's
sources. The shrew-taming story has folk and fabliaux
forebears; and the intrigue bred by the wooing of Bianca,
ancestors in Italian and Latin comedy rich in deceived
fathers, clever servants, and ridiculous pedants—as many
students have noted. The blending of materials surpasses
that in *A Shrew* and aligns the play with *The Comedy of
Errors* in constructive skill.

The quality of the farcical in *The Shrew* has often been
commented on. E. K. Chambers draws a distinction
between farcical comedy that turns upon a complication
of intrigue and absurdity of incident (like the Bianca story)
and farcical comedy that turns upon the absurdity of bourgeois speech and manners (the Petruchio-Kate story and
that of *The Merry Wives of Windsor*). He argues that the
primary dramatic interest of the latter is still character,
as in most conventional comedy, whatever elements of
intrigue or buffoonery may be woven into it. He holds
it comedy of the market-place; that is, comedy "translated
from the speech and manners of cultivated society into
the speech and manners of the *bourgeoisie*"; or, put with
more historical accuracy, comedy of the speech and manners of cultivated society is a development out of farce
by a "sharpening of the wits and the refinement of the
moral issues which accompany or form part of the growth
of a cultivated society as distinct from a *bourgeoisie*. Such
farce is a comedy of the ruder vices and the more robust
virtues, a comedy in which fisticuffs, literal and verbal,
take the place of rapier-play."⁶ Traceable to the very dawn
of the history of drama, it is not primarily a drama of
incident and intrigue but of a definite outlook upon life
just as truly as high comedy itself is. However, its outlook

is cynical and brutal rather than sympathetic or ironical. It presents an extravagant or burlesque perversion of the normal instead of a merely humorous or whimsical arrangement of it, and is more universal than fine comedy that demands "a quick-witted urban folk, trained in the arena of the *salon* to applaud the give-and-take of dialogue and to discern nice shades in the surface of things."[7] It sounds no Meredithian "silvery laughter"; it is often coarse and obscene. The stock-in-trade of the mimes of late classical times, it appeared in exuberance in the fourteenth century, was close akin to medieval fabliaux, and passed, Chambers holds, into Shakespeare's times through the farce of the English drama of the early sixteenth century that competed with didactic allegory. Such bourgeois "farce of character" likes always stock stuff: the tricks of trades in bad repute, the warfare between townsmen and clerks, the greed and hypocrisy of friars and priests, the ingenious wiles of rogues like Autolycus, and above all the duel of sex as matrimony often aggravates it. Beaten wives, henpecked husbands, cuckolds, and shrews are among its oldest conventionalized characters, as I have noted.[8] Yet there are too many crisscrossings of intrigue, absurd incident, and bumptious or brutally funny characterization—types and more types from classical times—not to grant great fluidity to the term farce. My chief point is the constant presence in all of it of the abrupt clash in the moment between animal actuality and accrued forms and conventions, little modified by what I have understood as humor or by any other kin of the comic. *The Shrew* illustrates farce turning upon the interminable tug-of-war between male and female egos getting yoked in holy matrimony for the sake of posterity. Its farcical absurdities are familiar to all of us, particularly if we happen to bear that yoke.

Perhaps no human relationship or "convention" has inspired so much radically comic creation as the matrimonial. By instinct the human rooster is perhaps no more monogamous than his barnyard brother; nor is the human Pertelote averse to various Chaunticleers. Over the ages we have laughed at the absurd clashes of the marriage bond with animal fact, at the endless duel for "maiestrye" within the bond or for freedom to slip out of it—at beaten wives, henpecked husbands, and cuckolds. Browbeaten husbands in an audience still get vicarious pleasure out of Petruchio's taming of his particular hell-cat—witness "Kiss Me, Kate," which gives the theme a modern flip. Katherina's cuffing of Petruchio, their verbal abuse of each other, his preposterous ways with her on their wedding day—killing "her in her own humour" (IV.i.183)—finally make her cry

> And be it moon, or sun, or what you please.
> And if you please to call it a rush candle,
> Henceforth I vow it shall be so for me.   (IV.v.13–15)

All are acts that amuse by abruptly turning the conventional conduct of lovers upside-down, by violently contrasting basic urges with conventional norms. Of course neither Petruchio nor Katherina is portrayed in depth, yet there is great verve and playhouse persuasiveness about both. Katherina in being given a damnable temper is made to seem to deserve something of the educational program Petruchio proceeds to knock her through—at least to prejudiced male judges who surely did most of the applauding in the public playhouse of London. We are free to fancy that there is a pert twinkle in the eyes of the shrew when she vows that they will see what her master orders them to see, and so wins from him by her absurd docility, "Why, there's a wench! Come on and kiss me, Kate" (V.ii.180). We suspect that she will know how to humor her lord so as to be the heart of his household, whatever illusions he may have about himself as its head. Such farcical stuff has been strong meat for sentimentalists and feminists, with none of whom Shakespeare had to reckon. Students have noted that he does

keep the fun above the coarse level of fabliaux cousins
of the shrew-taming story and that there is a certain
delicacy in his way with Katherina on her honeymoon
in contrast with what might have been expected. Yet she
remains no more than a lively and exasperating shrew
tamed by the end, credible enough in a farce comedy
in popular playhouse when nobody had ever dreamed
of votes for women or of Ibsen and Shaw taking up the
cudgel to champion their rights. Ultimate folly in reading
the role is to fancy for a second that Ann Hathaway
inspired it.

I leave certain strains in *The Shrew* to glance at the third
farce, *The Merry Wives of Windsor* (about 1600), another
instance of what Chambers would have us call bourgeois
farce of the market-place. As in *The Shrew,* the base plot
of the chaste wife who plays a trick on her would-be
seducer stems from old and widely spread folk tales, vari-
ants of which appear in Elizabethan literature and in
Italian—one in a popular ballad. We are still in that old
and favorite domain of popular farce: man's sportive amorousness clashing with society's marriage bond. Complex-
ities in the action carry the play into the category of comedy
of domestic intrigue, one might argue. But Chambers discerningly sees this bourgeois farce of the market-place
as essentially acted fabliau—the best specimen in English
drama even as the tales by Chaucer's Reve and Miller
are the best fabliaux in English narrative verse. As Chambers observes, the play has all the well-known earmarks
of the genre: "the realistic portraiture of contemporary
types; the frankness, not to say coarseness, of manners;
the light esteem for the marriage-tie; and the love of
'scoring-off' some one, and by preference in a matter of
venery."[9] Whatever the discrepancies and imperfections
in the plotting that some critics have balked before, the
play abounds in the vitality and verve of animal life overflowing the dams of convention. The two central scenes
wherein the buckbasket is pivotal have the vivacity of

rough and tumble action that marks the farcical at its best; and the intrigue has a drive reminiscent of *The Comedy of Errors*.

A word about the characterization to which the farcical incidents contribute. Sentimental critics have shuddered before Falstaff, now freight for a buckbasket and now dumped into a dirty ditch, as if Shakespeare were not sole owner of 'this creation of imagination all compact and free to do with him what time and occasion and his own pleasure and profit dictated.[10] Of course this Falstaff is not the matchless wit and humorist of the Henry plays. Could he well have remained that and become the butt of practical joking in a broad farce designed probably to tickle the vigorous tastes of a virgin queen who would relish the jolly outwitting of an old lecher, presumptuously wooing at once two honest matrons while he kept his eye on their cash? Elizabeth's way with loose love at court was far from tolerant even when favorites like Ralegh offended. Hazelton Spencer was surely right in declaring that in this fabliau-farce Falstaff was bound to come a cropper, but that, even so, he is still genial and lovable in his rascality and not out-talked even by a Welsh preacher.[11] And surely the other characters have variety and life enough for the farce of incident and intrigue that they figure in. In murdering English for our amusement, Evans and Caius confront us with a stock figure in comedy—the outlandish foreigner who mishandles the home words so as to contrast them absurdly with what the natives expect. The amusement afforded is very like that given by puns; indeed, the foreigner's mispronunciations are unconscious puns wherein one member of a pair of words similar in sound is a nonentity that misses the mark except insofar as the native can surmise the target shot for. Such surface amusement is particularly at home in farce in which the fun keeps to the ridiculousness of this or that in the extant moment as it collides with the conventional. The two merry wives have solidity enough for playhouse plausibility in farce; and Ford is nicely humanized to key with the jolly finale by his good fellowship in it and honest confession of his former folly. Slender, an amusing simpleton drawn in one dimension, is perfectly illustrative of the way a farcical character that calls for only surface strokes yet comes alive in Shakespeare's hands.

To look longer at the three farce comedies that I have reviewed would be to see more than the farcical strains that dominate in them. The romantic mingled with the comic is before us.

CHAPTER III

The COMIC and
the ROMANTIC INTERMINGLED:
The Two Gentlemen of Verona

Bold enough to try to describe the comic and its kin, I am not rash enough to attack both the romantic and the poetic, terms unavoidable in studying strains of the comic in Shakespeare's plays. I shall venture a word about the former term and leave my reader with his own understanding of the later. Santayana may first be heard on the nature of romance:

> I don't know whether its springs should be called Celtic or Norse or simply primitive and human, or whether any subtle currents from Alexandria or Arabia, or from beyond, swelled the flood in the dark ages. Suffice it that Romance is something very old, and supplies that large element which is neither classical nor Christian in mediaeval and modern feeling. It lies deeper, I think, in most of us than any conventional belief or allegiance. It involves a certain sense of homelessness in a chaotic world, and at the same time a sense of meaning and beauty there. To Romance we owe the spirit of adventure; the code of honour, both masculine and feminine; chivalry and heraldry; feudal loyalty; hereditary nobility; courtesy, politeness, and pity; the love of nature; rhyme and perhaps lyric melody; imaginative love and fidelity; sentimentality; humour. Romance was a great luminous mist blowing from the country into the ancient town; in the wide land of Romance everything was vaguely placed

and man migratory; the knight, the troubadour, or the palmer
carried all his permanent possessions on his back, or in his
bosom. So did the wandering student and the court fool.
There was much play with the picturesque and the miraculous;
perhaps the cockiness of changing fashions has the same
source. Fancy has freer play when men are not deeply respectful to custom or reason, but feel the magic of strangeness
and distance, and the profound absurdity of things.[1]

Much in this passage (not untouched by the poetic) suggests romantic elements in Shakespeare's comedies; the
words "humour" and "absurdity" in it would link the
romantic tightly to the comic.

Romance is obviously a word of many facets. I shall
let it refer to that rich body of medieval song and story,
its roots old and obscure, wherein idealizing love and
marvelous adventure in distant lands mingled in many
proportions. In Renaissance times its amorous strain,
inseparable from chivalric courtly love, was modified by
revived Platonic idealism and Petrarchan sonneteering.
Chaucer's *Knight's Tale* and *Sir Gawain and the Green
Knight*, those finest flowers of English metrical romances,
beautifully illustrate much that is essential in traditional
romance; so do Sidney's *Arcadia* and, of course, Shakespeare's own romantic comedies. Now the romantic so
understood offers an invitation to the comic in easily flying
away from brute fact. Shakespeare's comic genius early
divined in romance a fertile field in which to range. The
marvel of the romantic comedies is that the comic spirit
in them repeatedly deflates the excesses of romantic love
and adventure and yet leaves true love and noble action
more admirable than ever because somehow saner and
sweeter for the comic infusion.

Into the early *The Comedy of Errors* threads of such
romance are significantly woven:

His Plautine material is in the boisterous, gross, realistic pattern of Latin comedy: a virago of a wife, a thick-skinned
husband, and a common courtesan.... But into this
Hogarthian group Shakespeare slips one or two figures who

belong to another world: an old man weighed down by the grief of many years' fruitless search for the wife and for the son torn from him by shipwreck, and a gentle-hearted girl whose lips speak in the sweet new style singers and sonneteers were consecrating to lovers and to love-making. . . . The plot of the *Comedy of Errors* is Roman, classical, realistic; but old Ægeon and fair Luciana are the offspring of an un-Roman, unclassical and unrealistic sentiment: they are the outcome of romance. Of the two, Luciana is the more significant.[2]

She foreshadows the ladies of the mature romantic comedies and inspires in the Syracusan Antipholus lyric verses (III.ii. 47–51) that anticipate the adoring voices of Orlando and Orsino.

In Bianca and her suitors in *The Shrew* there also flows some of this blood of romance. Now this stuff of Latin-Renaissance farce on the side of mere narrative is not unknown to the far-flung net of romantic story; what signifies is Shakespeare's treatment of it. H. B. Charlton marks the slight shifts toward sentiment that Ariosto makes in delineating the principals in the Bianca story; with him the "germ of romanticism is beginning to leaven the classical tradition." The heroine is growing toward Rosalind, Beatrice, and Viola, "the very incarnation of the spirit of Shakespeare's comedy." Indeed, "the history of sixteenth-century comedy in Europe is a record of the encroachment of romance on the ancient domain of comedy" in which love is distinctly not romanticized. The adaptations of the English translators "in almost every respect . . . excise the more squalid and unromantic episodes of the original, to convert the story into a romantic play of love, rivalry and reconciliation." In *A Shrew* there is "artistically the crudest kind of medley. . . . its wooing plot is in the most flagrant or even fatuous romantic manner. . . . There is . . . nothing to impede the steady flow of high falutin' literary devotion. . . . Every comic incident of its original in Ariosto is either dropped or clumsily perverted to a use which enlarges the fatuous romanticism of its dominant temper."[3]

"There is a far finer dramatic instinct in Shakespeare's *Taming of the Shrew*. Bianca is never set adrift in the wide ocean of romantic emotion. . . . her wooers are deprived of the licence, so riotously enjoyed by those in *The Taming of a Shrew*, to dissolve their sugary hearts in luscious volubility. . . . Love remains more an intrigue than a religion. Hence the convenience of the classical machinery. Wily, scheming men-servants, disguises to procure mistaken identifications, inopportune coincidences to be encountered by still further reaches of unfeeling cunning—these are the traditional weapons of classical comedy."[4] Yet if Lucentio "is enthralled when he sees her coral lips to move" and finds "the very air about her is perfumed by her breath," the wooers of Bianca do not "dissolve their sugary hearts in luscious volubility" as do the wooers in *A Shrew*.[5] *The Taming of the Shrew* on the side of the Bianca story is traditional farce merely touched with romance, not comedy transformed by it as in Shakespeare's romantic comedies toward which I move.

The romantic strain in *The Merry Wives* is obviously the love tale of "sweet Anne Page" and "young Master Fenton" that fans out over the last scene of the comedy. If romantic in a lowered, bourgeois key, their love story does point toward the mature romantic comedies; and farcical Herne the Hunter in Windsor Forest foreshadows Bottom in his fairyland one. E. K. Chambers has written felicitously of the romantic and poetic quality of the last scene:

> Out of the busy Windsor streets, with their eating and mirth and laughter, . . . [Shakespeare] steps into the dewy glades where the shadows of legendary oaks lie black across the white moonlight. A gross form wearing the horns and clanking the chains of Herne the Hunter lies prostrate in a ditch, while the light-footed children flit amongst the trees with torches that glimmer like fireflies. And for a moment the mockery and malice give way to romance, as sweet Anne Page, eluding alike him who would take her in white and him who would take her in green, trips disguised in red

to where the priest awaits her with young Master Fenton, who has kept company, it is whispered, with the wild prince and Poins, but is an honest lad for all that—'he capers, he dances, he has eyes of youth, he writes verses, he speaks holiday, he smells April and May.'[6]

Farcical Falstaff and the romantic young lovers—all the folk—literally join hands in the happy harmony of the end as Mrs. Page cries:

> let us every one go home
> And laugh this sport o'er by a country fire,
> Sir John and all.   (V.v.255–257)

We may well recall Heywood on comedy as compounded of "sportfull accidents" and "foolish inamorates . . . merrily fitted for the stage . . . to recreate . . . or to refresh" us by laughter.

Now that we have met the radically comic and the romantic and the poetic interwoven in three plays predominantly farcical, I turn to *The Two Gentlemen of Verona*, a romantic comedy that fails to achieve the harmony of the comic and romantic and all other strains that does come in the plays that follow it. For most moderns this play is so top-heavy with the romantic that it collapses into comic absurdity in its denouement. Yet the old materials that Shakespeare adapts embrace even more of the stock stuff of romance, as students of them in Jorge de Montemayor's *Diana* well know. In the Spanish romance, however, there is no Valentine, no love versus friendship theme such as climaxes Shakespeare's play. Whatever the differences between source and play, the latter is crammed with the stock and trade of romance: lovers crossed and double-crossed, a loving maiden disguised as a man and pursuing her beloved, a rope ladder and flight from a tyrannical father, exile, outlaws in a greenwood, a serenade with ironic overtones, a rendezvous at a friar's cell, a ring for a token, attempted rape and theatrical rescue, and at last forgiveness all around with a big dash

of heroics. Drawn from *Diana*—from the very air of sonneteering Elizabethan England—is the idealizing or idoliz-
ing of the beloved that I have marked as central in the
romantic; with such love the play is supersaturated.[7] Lyrical passages throughout it radiate romantic love: it
dominates Valentine; even false Proteus illustrates its vio-
lation. Channeled into friendship, it brings the climax
of a play weak in exposition and driving action—and a
resolution of complications before which most of us balk:

> *Val.*   Now I dare not say
> I have one friend alive: thou wouldst disprove me.
> Who should be trusted when one's own right hand
> Is perjured to the bosom? Proteus,
> I am sorry I must never trust thee more
> But count the world a stranger for thy sake.
> The private wound is deepest. O time accurst,
> 'Mongst all foes that a friend should be the worst!
>   *Pro.* My shame and guilt confounds me.
> Forgive me, Valentine. If hearty sorrow
> Be a sufficient ransom for offence,
> I tender't here. I do as truly suffer
> As e'er I did commit.
>   *Val.*   Then I am paid;
> And once again I do receive thee honest.
> Who by repentance is not satisfied
> Is nor of heaven nor earth; for these are pleas'd;
> By penitence th' Eternal's wrath 's appeas'd.
> And, that my love may appear plain and free,
> All that was mine in Silvia I give thee.   (V.iv.65–83)

We may remember that Elizabethan audiences fed on
the sensational in romantic story; we may remember their
Christian exaltation of repentance and forgiveness; we
may remember that a comedy is privileged to end without
logical tidiness in its story and fidelity to life in its characters; and we may remember the Renaissance exaltation
of friendship between man and man as surpassing his
love for woman—but these speeches will not go down

today. The Elizabethan "frame of reference" and easy way with the finale of a comedy may have saved the scene in Shakespeare's theater as nothing nowadays will. We ask if Valentine would forgive so promptly; we think it preposterous that he yields up Silvia thus. Character portrayed with strict psychological fidelity is not the primary concern of the dramatist, as E. E. Stoll repeatedly reminded us; it is situation so manipulated as to move an audience to tears or laughter, to enthrall and transport it. But in these speeches by Valentine and Proteus we feel facts undercutting such artistic probability as a dramatist must respect more than mere possibility. For us the romantic suddenly slips into the absurd, into the radically comic realm where rough animal actuality by abruptly confronting romantic conventions of love and friendship makes them ridiculous. Suddenly the romantic turns farcical. Because the romantic has "called the tune of *The Two Gentlemen of Verona*, and governed the direction of the action of the play,"[8] Valentine and Proteus go comic for us in an ironic way that their creator, close to the age of romance, surely never intended that they should. For us the "conventions" by which Valentine lives

> involve him in [sic] most ridiculous plight.... The hero of romantic comedy appears no better than its clowns.... Thurio ... was cast for the dotard of the play, and of course he is not without egregious folly. But what was meant in the end to annihilate him with contempt, turns out quite otherwise. Threatened by Valentine's sword, he resigns all claim to Silvia, on the ground that he holds him but a fool that will endanger his body for a girl that loves him not. The audience is invited to call Thurio a fool for thus showing himself to be the one person in the play with a modicum of worldly wisdom, a respect for the limitations of human nature, and a recognition of the conditions under which it may survive. Clearly, Shakespeare's first attempt to make romantic comedy had only succeeded so far that it had unexpectedly and inadvertently made romance comic.[9]

For us the outlaws of the play are like "the Pirates of Penzance: but then Gilbert meant his to be funny."[10] Such is man's shifting way with the realm of the comic which turns upon just how in any given society conventions are taken vis-à-vis the animal base that breeds them.

In Julia and Launce good sense checks romantic sensibility run riot. Ladies in traditional romance are, with certain exceptions like the Green Knight's lady, notoriously colorless; the "code allowed to woman no duty but to excite by her beauty the devoted worship of her knight." But "Julia is a creation, not a convention." She "is depicted in moods, whimsies, and vagaries which are in fact the stuff of dramatic characterisation"; she has " 'no other but a woman's reason, I think him so because I think him so.' "[11] If Proteus seems to us a sorry fellow upon whom to lavish her love, the woman in her knows, as we should, that love is blind. Her common sense, except in her choice of her love, is nicely illustrative of the way the critically comic looks behind the forms and conventions of society to the honest impulses beneath them.

Launce and Speed are, of course, instruments with which the comic cuts down the desiccated wood of romance around them. They bring us face to face with the Elizabethan clown or fool, whose mixed ancestry Touchstone perhaps best reveals. If Speed "belongs to the purely theatrical family of the Dromios, with their punning and logic-chopping asininities,"[12] Launce is kin to the native Costard of *Love's Labour's Lost* and to numerous rustic clowns whose earthy naturalness clashes with the social sophistications around them. This particular "country bumpkin" sort of clown gives us comic monologues that, so G. L. Kittredge thought, "have never been surpassed." "The quibbling dialogues, which remind one of *Love's Labour's Lost* and *The Comedy of Errors*, are good of their kind, but not extraordinary. They show the influence of Lyly and follow a classical convention to which Shakespeare was, of course, obedient at the outset of his career."[13] Charlton points out that Launce's comic worth, as compared with Speed's and with that of the Dromios, is admirably indicated by the way Launce makes consummate use of Speed's curiosity and of his better schooling. Launce gets his letter deciphered, displays his own superior breeding, and maneuvers the "boy's correction." "Launce is happiest with his dog. Clownage can go no farther than the pantomimic representation, with staff and shoe and dog, of the parting from his home-folks. Laughter is hilarious at Launce's bitter grief that his ungrateful cur declined to shed a tear. That Launce should expect it is, of course, the element of preposterous incongruity which makes him a clown."[14]

Following our concept of the radically comic, we see the essence of such clownage in the absurd clash between the basic facts of man as an animal and his forms and conventions shifted by Launce into one between the instincts of dumb animals and man's manners—between a dog's life and man's conventions for covering his own animal nature. Over long time radical comedy has exploited such material; witness Chaucer's chickens and Thurber's dogs. When Launce's dog treats a lady's farthingale as he would any tree trunk, he pitches the contrast between dog-fact and man-propriety into the excretory realm, in which masters of the radically comic like Aristophanes and Rabelais and Chaucer have always sported. Nothing so jars man's conventions of propriety like abruptly confronting them with excretory and sexual facts. "Mannekin-Pis," that Mecca for provincial tourists in Brussels, grows in radically comic stature the more formally he is attired by sportive townspeople. Even as Launce expects of his dog more pity than is by nature in a dog, so romance expects more of Valentine and Proteus than it is in the essential nature of man to be; and they collapse into something less than man. In giving up his cur, Launce makes as great a sacrifice as does Valentine himself—but "the effect hardly suggests that self-sacrifice is worldly-wise. And so once more it seems to bring into question the worldly worth of the code that sanctifies such deeds. Unintentionally, Launce has become the means by which the incompatibilities and the unrealities of romantic postulates are laid bare."[15] He "sharpens our appreciation of the particular range of incongruities which are the province of comedy—the incongruity between what a thing really is and what it is taken to be."[16]

The quibbling dialogue of the play, echoing like stuff in *The Comedy of Errors*, anticipates the word play in *Love's Labour's Lost*. But the wit—puns and all—is thin stuff beside the abundance of it in that later play. Although the lyricism is in a stock romantic vein, at moments that of the Sonnets is suggested, and the last scene opens with a fine poetic soliloquy by Valentine ("How use doth breed a habit in a man!").

In his earliest venture (it would seem) into romantic comedy, Shakespeare does not harmonize the comic and the romantic. Improbabilities in action, inherent in romance, make unintentionally absurd or comic—at least for us today—crucial conduct by Valentine and Proteus, persuasive though Julia and Launce be. For some tastes Launce is more comic than Launcelot Gobbo in *The Merchant of Venice;* Julia speaks to Lucetta (I.ii.) so as to forecast Portia and Nerissa (I.ii.); and Julia disguised in service to Proteus anticipates Viola disguised in service to Orsino in *Twelfth Night*. Julia's plea to Silvia for Proteus and her speechless love for her master look toward the Viola-Orsino-Olivia triangle, which will blend superbly the romantic, the poetic, the humorous, the pathetic, and the ironic. Far less potent in comic qualities than *The Comedy of Errors, The Taming of the Shrew*, and *The Merry Wives of Windsor, The Two Gentlemen of Verona* is yet a revealing bridge (one often noted) into the mature plays that fuse comic, romantic, and all other strains.

CHAPTER IV

The COMIC and
the ROMANTIC INTEGRATED:
From *Love's Labour's Lost*
through *The Tempest*

Love's Labour's Lost, the first comedy fully to harmonize the comic and the romantic, is based on a radically comic situation: the determination of the King of Navarre and his three lords to dictate to Cupid by putting books before beddings. The treatment is often called satiric; yet so without bite is it that we see anew the thin line between the satiric and the critically comic.[1] The play is supersaturated in wit.

An easy approach to such aspects of the play is to review its manipulation of its radically comic situation act by act. All students grant the thinness of the story and the meagerness of dramatic incident; however, though "slight, the plot suffices to keep things moving. Our interest centres not in the action but in the delightfully whimsical situation; and the eccentricities of that situation are managed with consummate skill, set forth vividly in ironic characterization, and illuminated by polished wit in dialogue and soliloquy."[2] For one fresh from *The Two Gentlemen*, the play does begin with relative swiftness. In its first two scenes the agreement of the king and his nobles to forswear ladies for three years of study is set before us. The seizure of Costard and Jaquenetta for breach of the proclamation forbidding a youth to be "taken with a wench" and Armado's confession that he is himself smitten with sudden love for one at once bode ill for the radically comic resolve of the aristocrats, even as Berowne's quick skepticism about the life of men without women foreshadows the debacle ahead. In the second act comes the comic collapse of the males upon meeting irresistible females. But there is no movement forward in complication for high or low characters until Berowne near the end of the third act arranges with Costard to carry his love-letter to Rosaline. Except for that letter, this act with its fooling and amusing characterization that runs to the exaggeration of caricature is something of a dead center in point of suspense. The next act moves along somewhat better, though its first two scenes are hardly dramatic: graceful talk with ingenious repartee leads into Costard's mistake in presenting to the princess Don Armado's letter to Jaquenetta, though little is made of the farcical mistake and the scene ends with much mere badinage on wholly different subjects; then in the next scene Berowne's letter, which Jaquenetta has received, is half-forgotten in the quibbling and pedantic patter of Holofernes, Sir Nathaniel, and Dull. The third scene gives an excellent farcical sequence in the successive entrances of the king, Longaville, and Dumain, each thinking he confesses his love in secret, only to be overheard by each of the men who has preceded him—all, except Berowne, wholly unaware of the presence of the others. The sequence is capped by the wench's delivering Berowne's letter; it compels him to comic confession of his hypocrisy in scoffing at his fellow-lovers. The successive situations, farcical and ironic, illustrate an ancient comic device—the "trickster tricked." The effect here is that of surprise box within surprise box except that the audience expects the suprise although those tricked do not.

This multiplication of farcical effect is not unlike that arising from doubled twins in *The Comedy of Errors*.

Involved is the artistic principle explicated by Charles Morgan and stressed in turn by E. E. Stoll as the source of much effectiveness in drama: suspense of form as against suspense of plot. "Suspense of form is the excited expectation not of the answer to a puzzle, or of the disclosure of a mystery, but—under the spell of illusion—of the the rounding out of a harmony, like the rime to come at the end of a verse or the rest tone at the end of a song. It is the expectation of the way that Othello will receive the slander and afterwards the truth, or that Hamlet will baffle his enemies, have his revenge and meet his death."[3] Here the expectation that each lover will be "hoist with his own petar" is taken in radically comic stride, though of course suspense of form, granted a milieu of disastrous enmeshment, can be equally potent in formal tragedy. The principle is perhaps fundamental in any art form; certainly in music we expect the fulfilment of a design as its fore part builds toward the satisfying completion of it. Stoll notes that "suspense of form" invites irony more than does suspense of plot—irony not only of the retrospective sort but of the prospective sort. We know the facts as the characters do not and hence foresee their logical resolution as they cannot. Comic drama is shot through with such ironic suspense. It affords scope for the radical contrast between fact and fiction that is at the heart of the comic. Undoubtedly the Elizabethan sophisticates for whom the play was obviously written relished having Cupid's converted votaries praise the beauties of their respective ladies only to be trumped by Berowne—himself immediately and ironically trumped by the move of a mere serving wench.

Little appears left for the fifth act except such comedy as may arise from Don Armado's letter in the hands of the princess. Hence we at once get promise of fresh comic complications from a masquerading visit by the smitten gentlemen to the "girls of France"; we get, too, another fresh line of comic interest in the announcement that

Holofernes and his friends will enact "The Nine Worthies" before the princess and her attendants. If not an organic outgrowth of earlier action, the visit does promise comic turns for romantic moves; and the playlet, deflation of romanticized dignitaries. Shortly we are laughing at the farcical situations that disguises breed. In multiplying fictions to cover facts, disguise multiplies occasions for comic clashes between the actual and the apparent; no wonder it is abidingly present in comedy. The clashes in this area of the play are kept to the radically comic level in that characterization is never in depth and no criticism is voiced or implicit. Romantic wooing is given farcical turns. Farcical, too, is the enactment of "The Nine Worthies" by asinine eccentrics disguised as great ancients for the amusement of romantic lovers—Costard as director flipping the performance the while he tosses off Pompey the Great as his bit. The final stretch of the play is rich enough in lively incident, variety, and surprise when Mercade brings news that clouds a comedy that yet rightly ends with a merry song.

If the radically comic and the comically ironic give the base of the play, "polished wit in dialogue and soliloquy" most distinguishes it. When Shakespeare began writing about 1590, John Lyly of *Euphues* fame was still the chief comic dramatist for the city sophisticates—their reigning stylist. Over the preceding decade his two novels and his court comedies of slight plot and much graceful, witty talk by amorous characters in various romantic postures, yet never drawn in depth, were in vogue with the fashionable folk who gravitated around the court of Elizabeth. Euphuism was a style marked by formal parallelism and antithesis in structure, elaborate and patterned alliteration, and decorative allusions to "unnatural natural history," to classical mythology, and to the lives of the Greeks and Romans—all so mixed by Lyly that witty word manipulation was constant and deliberate. Though far beyond Lyly's powers in poetic and natural touches in characterization, *Love's Labour's Lost* is Shakespeare's half-emulative, half-mocking venture into Lyly's domain. On the count of sheer verbal ingenuity Shakespeare would out-Lyly Lyly, so to say. Obviously Shakespeare has absorbed, digested, and transcended him and so can laugh at the excesses and affectations of the Euphuistic manner the while he creates his own uniquely witty comedy in its wake. Even most of the low comic characters (with prototypes in Lyly) are wits in their fashion. As Shakespeare in his scintillating word-game outplays his model, he yet laughs at all affectations and pedantry; he will spin out a pseudo-Euphuistic dialogue, then wheel around and parody himself and his model. The unfailing verve of his word juggling captivates us. In breeding delight in itself within the extant moment, such wit is essentially in key with the radically comic situations that are the groundwork of the play. And most of the time the wit is the vehicle for exposing the absurdities of romantic love. A supreme master of words is running his scales this way and that, acquiring that full felicity with which he will manipulate language in the mellowest of his romantic comedies and the most moving of his tragedies. Our pleasure in the verbal brilliance of the play is akin to that given us by the virtuosity of finished clowning or juggling; it is pleasure in sheer dexterity in a skill within the moment and heedless of any complications past or to come. Such verbal brilliance is the right milieu for lords and ladies and king and princess who are graceful and charming puppets for projecting the radically comic situations in which natural needs topple foolish pretenses. Of course such characters lack depth and are artificial if we put them beside Falstaff and Juliet's nurse—but we should not. The tone of the play is exquisitely artificial and the characters are simply in key. The ladies play the love-game with easy grace and charm, certain of themselves and of victory in rebuking comical absurdities in egotistical males. If men are more often comic figures than women, it is perhaps because they are normally more often assertive and strike more rigid stances than do women, who keep their ears closer to mother earth. Fussy Pertelote is funny; strutting Chaunticleer is funnier. Even the names of comic males in Shakespeare often suggest their absurdities: Bottom, Dogberry, Pistol, Slender, Sir Toby Belch, Sir Andrew Aguecheek, and Dull. Doll Tearsheet is as deliciously named as Fielding's Slipslop; but most ladies in the comedies bear neutral names: Katherina, Portia, Silvia, Julia, Rosalind, Viola, and the Princess of France, Rosaline, Maria, and Katherine in the play before us. Nature is on the side of those last four ladies against the ridiculous resolve of the gentlemen to turn their backs on Venus *genetrix*, mother of us all, and pay their devotions to books alone. Lovers in absurd or romantic postures may invite the rebuke of satire; yet what they get is so without any moral indignation, so crossed with the radically comic, the tolerantly humorous, and the persistently witty even among their low class associates that the chastisement given folly is only mildly if not meekly satiric.

Although Shakespeare moves beyond Lyly in casting his romantic love among plausible men and women, not mythological or allegorical figures, the passion of love is in their speech only in flashes; in the main they are pretty figurines to subserve the central satirical point and harmonize with the world of wit in which they gracefully live. Berowne and the Princess and Rosaline have moments of actuality, but it is among the low characters that the comic takes on flesh and blood.

Costard, Jaquenetta, and Armado as a love triangle contrast comically with the double quadrangle of aristocratic lovers and in their solidity underpin them; in their bald amorousness they underscore the comic absurdity of the pretenses of the quartet of romantic gentlemen. The central situation given mildly satiric treatment is farcical in being radically at odds with animal need. The upshot of this treatment emerges in the sanely romantic strain heard in Berowne's lines:

> From women's eyes this doctrine I derive.
> They sparkle still the right Promethean fire;
> They are the books, the arts, the academes,
> That show, contain, and nourish all the world.
> Else none at all in aught proves excellent.   (IV.iii.350–354)

Reflected in such verses is a tempering of the excessively romantic love that in *The Two Gentlemen of Verona* Launce and Speed could not singlehandedly give. Now a gentleman himself lends a hand. Such verses throw into comic perspective the conventional sonnets by the gentlemen that voice romantic love untempered by such sense—such humor. The mildly satiric and the critically comic fuse to bring sanity to the gentlemen, Berowne in particular; by their jolly farce comedy Costard and his associates indirectly nurture romantic maturity in them.

Costard, Jaquenetta, Armado, and their fellows stem from stock type characters of Latin and Italian comedy, particularly from *commedia dell'arte* ones: Costard, from the rustic clown; Jaquenetta, from the ill-favored wench, mate for the *capitano* that Armado represents; Moth, from the *zanni*; Holofernes, from the pedant; and Nathaniel, from the parasite or *affamato.* Life comes into the lot through such finely humorous strokes as mark the speeches of Costard when he is faced with Ferdinand's reading of Armado's pretentious letter that charges this "base minnow" with having seduced a wench:

> *Cost.* Me!
> *Ferd.* 'that unlettered small-knowing soul'—
> *Cost.* Me!
> *Ferd.* 'that shallow vassal'—
> *Cost.* Still me!
> *Ferd.* 'which, as I remember, hight Costard'—
> *Cost.* O, me!   (I.i.253–260)

The comic repetitiousness of Costard's "me" and the into-
nation of surprised discovery in the "O" are deliciously
humorous. And such blunt honesty about sluttery does
as much to "whip hypocrisy" about love as does lordly
Berowne, ironically guilty of what he whips.

The satiric—modified by wit without malice, by humor
and comic irony, by romance purged of excessive idealism,
and by lyric tones—also punctures pretentious speech out
of step with "russet yea's and honest kersey no's":

> Taffeta phrases, silken terms precise,
> Three-pil'd hyperboles, spruce affectation,
> Figures pedantical—these summer flies.   (V.ii.406–408)

Such "flies" blow all save Costard and Jaquenetta and
Dull more or less full of "maggot ostentation" even as
the vow to pursue celibacy and studies and so "cross the
cause why we were born" puffs up the king and the lords
for comic deflation. All the folk save these three have
a "mint of phrases" in their brains, though it is Armado's
minting head that is well broken for the lot of them when
he goes amorous with Jaquenetta:

> *Arm.* I do betray myself with blushing. Maid.
> *Jaq.* Man.
> *Arm.* I will visit thee at the lodge.
> *Jaq.* That's hereby.
> *Arm.* I know where it is situate.
> *Jaq.* Lord, how wise you are!
> *Arm.* I will tell thee wonders.
> *Jaq.* With that face?
> *Arm.* I love thee.
> *Jaq.* So I heard you say.
> *Arm.* And so farewell.
> *Jaq.* Fair weather after you!   (I.ii.138–149)

If the intent of wit be expert "verbal markmanship,"[4]
Jaquenetta is also infected in her fashion, for her completely flat and laconic retorts fell the ass Armado. Even
his plain speeches are undercut by her plainer retorts.

It is by such touches that the several type characters have some life breathed into them, come sufficiently alive in their radically comic functions to enhance the plausibility of the thinly portrayed highborn lovers who are juxtaposed to them. The technique is one that, appearing in *The Two Gentlemen* and completely mastered in *A Midsummer Night's Dream*, in all the mature comedies makes probable for the playhouse impossibly romantic or supernatural characters and situations: we think of the romantic lovers who rub shoulders with Bottom, Audrey, and Sir Toby.

The critically comic and the satiric fuse inextricably in *Love's Labour's Lost* to point up "mere necessity" as central in life and love, the wisdom of liking "of each thing that in season grows," and hostility to "flat treason 'gainst the kingly state of youth" when romance is in season.

> *Ber. For when would you, my lord, or you, or you,*
> *Have found the ground of study's excellence*
> *Without the beauty of a woman's face?* (IV.iii.299–301)

The upshot of the play is that we feel its author such "a perpetual fountain of good sense" as Dryden justly said Chaucer was—good sense that does not deny the validity of romantic love so long as it remembers it is tethered to vital needs. Chaucer and Shakespeare knew what Matthew Arnold, in spite of his pursuit of the other-worldly Celtic spirit, may have forgotten in praising Sophocles for his power to "see life steadily and see it whole": a sure way to miss beholding the best that life can reveal is to see it so steadily as to miss the idealizing love that can help us traverse its waste land.

Two other farcical situations in the play merit a glance: the double-crossing by the "girls of France" of the "Muscovites" come awooing and the ill-fated show of the Worthies put on by Armado and company. The former episode has that radical clash of appearance with fact in the moment that breeds the absurdity of every practical joke. A trick or a practical joke always involves an unex-

pected plunge from conventional life into the blind swirl
of existence and a quick emergence from it for the trickster,
if not for the tricked. So it is especially in sex jokes over
the ages. Tricks and jokes show how little character, with
its involutions spread over time and space, has to do with
the core of the comic that keeps to the things and events
behind all conventions. Tricks and jokes also reveal the
place of pure sportiveness in the comic, the playful meeting of the existential undercutting the conventional. Such
playfulness can run to annoying excess in the inveterate
joker; but a mature man's relish for a trick or joke hinges
on his readiness to accept the fact that life on the loose
largely eludes whatever net he can throw over it. He is
content to catch only the biggest fish and amused that
his petty five senses should aspire to catch more. The
joke played by the "girls of France" and clothed in scintillating wit teaches the gentlemen that

> The tongues of mocking wenches are as keen
> As is the razor's edge invisible,
> Cutting a smaller hair than may be seen,
> Above the sense of sense.   (V.ii.256–259)

Everybody "pecks up wit as pigeons pease" while the
joke runs its course to humble the gentlemen, already
"seasick, . . . coming from Muscovy." Then follows the
ridiculous burlesque of great Hector, Pompey, Alexander,
Hercules, and Judas Maccabæus by creatures as comically
petty in contrast with those dignitaries as any could be.[5]
With the voice of the authentic Shakespearean clown, Costard apologizes for Sir Nathaniel, collapsed as Alexander:
"He is a marvellous good neighbour, faith, and a very
good bowler; but as for Alisander—alas! you see how
'tis—a little o'erparted" (V.ii.586–589). Thus does humor
season the radically comic. Holofernes as Judas introduces
the pigmy Moth as Hercules in preposterous verse that
prettily reflects the pedantry of the speaker. Holofernes
is made the butt of farcical jibing that leaves him, literally,

shirtless. The jibes by the wits—sloughing off the "old rage" only "by degrees"—and the tempering sympathy for their butts voiced by the generous princess make a sequence to be repeated with more skill toward the finish of *A Midsummer Night's Dream* when Bottom and his fellows present "Pyramus and Thisbe" for spectators who playfully disparage the absurdities, the while we remember Theseus's generous words heard at the outset of the play:

> I will hear that play;
> For never anything can be amiss
> When simpleness and duty tender it. (V.i.81–83)

By just such interminglings of the sympathy, kindliness, and sufferance of humor, the brusqueness of the radically comic in Shakespeare is constantly tempered and the cutting edge of any satiric intent blunted.

The shadows that "begin to cloud" this last scene of the play when Mercade suddenly announces the death of the Princess's father have been held to show Shakespeare looking beyond the pretty patter of romantic wits to tragic depths yet to be plumbed. But those masculine egos are too incorrigibly witty not to need a sobering twelve months in which to learn to speak "honest plain words." Such shadows are illustrative of the way dark threads are woven into the mature comedies to suggest the full truth of life even as comic strains in the great tragedies do just that. Berowne cries: "Worthies away! The scene begins to cloud." Harley Granville-Barker has well written: "And it must seem to cloud; the gay colors fading out, the finery folding about the wearers like wings. But this is not the end, for the end must not be melancholy. The country folk have yet to sing and dance their antic; a little crowd of them, dressed to match the

> daisies pied and violets blue,
> And lady-smocks all silver white,
> And cuckoo-buds of yellow hue. . . .

"The comedy of affectation comes to its full close upon notes of pastoral freshness and simplicity."[6] The beautifully natural tone of the concluding song is most apt for ending a comedy that laughs at excessive wit and at any unnatural effort to deny Venus her primal rights—yet is itself infected. "It is surely no accident that the most verbally artificial and metrically elaborate of all Shakespeare's plays should end with the most rustic, simple and countrified of all his songs."[7] In gracefully juxtaposing the simple and sensuous delights of spring and winter in the country to all the pretenses of the fine folk of the play, the song caps it with a charmingly comic touch. Although the cuckoo already mocks the four married men to be, the last note we hear is a "merry" one from that wise old bird the owl. And an ultimate note it is in the realm of the comic uncrossed by anything else.

One final word about the mildly satirical strain in the play. Superficially looked at, that strain may seem dated in rebuking fads in speech and manners lost in time long past; but in its good-natured ridicule of man's pretenses to bridle nature by putting learning before the ladies, it holds abiding relevance. And even the verbal fireworks of the piece keep an appeal if we lend ears to the sheer fun of such ingenuity—an appeal not eclipsed by Joycean pyrotechnics in our own century. That spirit of fun in the flying moment is central in a comedy "pleasantly contrived with merry accidents, . . . intermixt with apt and witty jests," and "merrily fitted to the stage."

A Midsummer Night's Dream harmonizes the comic and its kin, the romantic, and the poetic with unique delicacy and grace; moreover, the supernatural, a realm that does not usually invite comic treatment, is enfolded within the comic compass; and song and dance happily crown all.

This superfine blending of diverse strains is paralleled by the fusion of various source materials: the Theseus-Hippolyta story treated in Chaucer's *Knight's Tale* and Plutarch's *Life of Theseus;* the Pyramus-Thisbe story at hand in Ovid; the love juice matched by magic potions in an episode in *Diana;* the fairy lore which Shakespeare and his audience absorbed in their childhood and found reflected in medieval and current tales and plays and pageants; the rustics with prototypes in the "hempen homespuns" of London and the countryside; and, many students think, a wedding festivity in aristocratic life that occasioned the writing of the play. Some such wedding in real life does appear to be tactfully figured in the Theseus-Hippolyta nuptial plans that frame the body of the play and set it moving. This royal romance envelops the four romantic lovers with whom the comic spirit sports in the forest, the fairies, and the "rude mechanicals," who in their "most lamentable comedy" unwittingly stand two famous tragic lovers on their heads to the amusement of all except themselves. The masque-like finale shows marital harmony restored between fairy king and queen and their blessing of the three pairs of lovers about to wed.

At the outset Theseus commands Philostrate to "awake the pert and nimble spirit of mirth" in celebrating the approaching marriage of the duke and the Amazonian queen. What event in man's seven ages so breeds jollity and happiness as a wedding wherein life is renewed in delight? Then social form and animal fact call a happy truce for a day, wryly tragic or comic though the day may appear in the after years. Puck is that "pert and nimble spirit of mirth" incarnate. He weaves the central farcical web for the exquisite fabric of the romantic comedy. This winged creature who can "put a girdle round about the earth / In forty minutes" (II.i.175–176) confesses that "those things do best please me / That befall prepost'rously" (III.ii.120–121)—love affairs ranging from Bottom's to Oberon's. Perhaps Theseus's amour is spared only because a compliment to a great lord is intended in that character. What doings in our lives repeatedly fall out more ridiculously than our amours? Where find more absurd clashes between instincts and conventions? Puck personifies the force that controls the arbitrary and absurd whirligig of love that sustains all animal life. As the manipulator of most of the intrinsically farcical events of the play, he represents the powers that mortals, half lost over time in the foggy crisscrosses of their loves, now curse for their cruel fate and now bless for their good luck. He gives a "local habitation and a name" to the irrationality of love, mother nature's blind way for the survival of our species. We lovers, like madmen, "have such seething brains, / Such shaping fantasies, that [we] apprehend / More than cool reason ever comprehends" and see "Helen's beauty in a brow of Egypt" (V.i.4–6,11). But our romantic flights, however high they soar, move on animal wings, and Puck, acutely aware of the absurd contrast between facts and fancies, shakes in laughter before it. Yet Puck himself is the mischievous agent of the fairy king. And Oberon and his retinue are essentially embodiments of the natural powers and influences that countless men and women, their ears close to earth, have fabricated over long time to give some shape to its mysteries.

Puck intervenes in the amours of all the romantic creatures of the play—tangling and untangling Lysander and Hermia, Demetrius and Helena, and even Oberon and Titania, and then blessing the union of Theseus and Hippolyta. This "pert and nimble spirit of mirth" plays fast and loose with Bottom and his fellows and their Pyramus and Thisbe. Into situations potentially tragic Puck plunges with "love in idleness." He pours into the eyes of sleeping Titania, who has defied the "maiestrye" of her lord, the magic juice to bring about her ridiculous enamourment with an ass. Oberon, overhearing Helena's vain pleadings with Demetrius for his love, orders a potion of the juice for his eyes so that he upon awakening will see Helena and fall in love with her. But Puck in a comic mistake anoints the eyes of Lysander. We smile in anticipation of the complications ahead—complications that follow immediately when Lysander awakes, sees Helena who has vainly pursued Demetrius, and begins to woo her with high romantic ardor. By the end of the scene Puck has reversed the original state of the lovers: Hermia, now forlorn and bereft, follows Lysander who in turn follows Helena, even as at the outset Helena had followed Demetrius who has pursued Hermia. Farcical situations pile up. In the next scene mischievous Puck, amid the absurd rustics, clamps an ass's head on Bottom to double the absurdity of his amour with Titania. And in the next scene, after Puck's amused rehearsal of his doings, comes the height of the farcical tangle for the four lovers when Oberon, discovering Puck's mistake, tries to rectify it by having him anoint the eyes of Demetrius and bring Helena before him when he awakes. We smile anew, for we know what neither Puck nor his master knows—that Lysander's sudden change to infatuation with Helena will breed confusion worse confounded if she is brought before Demetruis when he awakes: two lovers for Helena and none for Hermia where originally there had been none for Helena and two for Hermia. How better suggest the arbitrary, unfathomable, and absurd depths of nature from which events pop as she pleases, especially when she appears as Venus? Our sense of the irony in suspense of form is completed when Demetrius awakes and expectations of added entanglements are realized. We are free to be merely amused by the lively lovers' quarrel, for the "nimble spirit of mirth" now rampant assures us that Jill will yet get her right Jack. In leading the confused lovers with false calls under command of Oberon to rectify mistakes, Puck cries "this jangling I esteem a sport"—as indeed we do. Their jangling the audience found familiar, as who does not that knows how the path of true love runs? Finally Puck has all four lovers weary, lost in the fog (actual and amorous), and sleeping. Upon his squeezing the juice, aptly called "love in idleness," on Lysander's eyes the farcical-romantic story moves to its finish in which

Demetrius at last loves Helena and Lysander, wakened, once more loves Hermia.

A still finer stroke in Shakespeare's integration of the farcical and the romantic in the play is his having Puck maneuver even Oberon's dainty queen into loving an ass. Perhaps we may fancy that Bottom with his ass's head caressed in Titania's lap symbolizes the complete fusion of the farcical and the romantic. Perhaps we may even fancy Bottom animal man himself, calling for hay when Peaseblossom, Cobweb, Moth, and Mustardseed would serve a lover of the exquisite Titania, queen of the poetry of earth that is never dead and that surrounds him, even as they personify it. But in looking for the essence of two antipodean creatures, Puck and Bottom, and the quintessence of romance, Titania, one need not seek symbolic and allegorical patterns, fascinating though it be for moderns in their studies to ferret them out in the plays, often forgetful of the play as the thing in the theater.

The radically comic reins of the play now fall from Puck's magical hands to the horny ones of Nick Bottom, presenter and star of "The most Lamentable Comedy and most Cruel Death of Pyramus and Thisby." The contrast between these two manipulators is a finely comic one. The first has a knowing taste for the farcical; the latter unwittingly lives it and then as unwittingly enacts it. The very title of Bottom's play discloses the farcical essence of the thing —"most Lamentable Comedy and most Cruel Death" all in one package. The performance of it shows how the tragic turns into burlesque when reduced to flat facts and projected in a style that mocks the high heroic. We recall the presentation of lofty Hector, Pompey, Alexander, Judas Maccabaeus, and Hercules by lowly Armado, Costard, Sir Nathaniel, Holofernes, and Moth that also fructifies in travesty because specific elevated subjects are treated in a ridiculously trivial manner.[8] This burlesque of heroic-romantic love in the enchanted forest shows still again and from another angle what fools all lovers be.

Yet when this "palpable gross play hath well beguil'd / The heavy gait of night" (V.i.374–375), Theseus with gracious humor accepts it and at once looks toward "new jollity"; he yields to Puck and his fellows who "now are frolic"; and Puck yields to Oberon and Titania "with all their *Train*"—who sing and dance and bless the place before Puck pronounces the epilogue. In all is humorous sufferance of all absurdities; proliferating life such as the comic spirit delights in overflows in song and dance.

The fairies of ancient folk origin, central in the movement, rightly dominate the finish of a romantic comedy distinguished by most exquisite poetry. They are distillates of the natural world, constantly evoked by imagery reflective of the beauty and mystery of earth's flora and fauna. The fairies are made plausible by such imagery and, somehow, even by the bumpkins who smell of the same earth. Fairies, clowns, and images—sustained by verses always finally in key—buoy up the farcical mishaps of the lightly sketched romantic lovers, make them credible for the nonce.

A good yardstick for the harmony of the ingredients in this mature romantic comedy is a comparison with earlier comedies. The topsy-turvy tangles of the two pairs of lovers recall the mix-ups of the two sets of twins in *The Comedy of Errors;* but a mechanical baldness in the farcical in it has become a delicate and subtly motivated tangle of romantic lovers suggestive of the abiding arbitrariness of love in life. The radically comic and the romantic have been so fused that the asininities of Bottom and his crew seem utterly at ease beside the amours of their lofty betters. The ineptitudes of the romantic in *The Two Gentlemen*, which slipped unwittingly into the ridiculous at the finish, are now transcended by a touch that keeps a fine equipoise throughout in weaving a tissue of the farcical and the romantic. The integration of the Pyramus-Thisbe burlesque into the design of the play makes the performance of the Nine Worthies in *Love's Labour's Lost* seem a comic appendage. The burlesque is prepared for early in the play by Theseus's command to Philostrate and is akin to the amorous farce that Puck effects in the forest. Farcical and romantic elements in *The Taming of the Shrew* seem coarse and divergent by the side of the deft and fresh ways for integrating them in the *Dream.* Wit rings its targets but never seems a volley of bird-shot more or less for its own sake as it often does in *Love's Labour's Lost.* And the pervasive poetic beauty of the play is immeasurably finer than anything that has preceded it.

Pervasive humor, too, is perhaps best seen in the character of Theseus, in his kindness and sufferance of the absurdities of the rustics:

> Our sport shall be to take what they mistake;
> And what poor duty cannot do, noble respect
> Takes it in might, not merit.   (V.i.90–92)

Nowhere is there an intent to correct or reform mere mortals, to rebuke or chastise. The farcical and the humorous dominate a play devoid of the correctively comic and the satiric. If Theseus focuses the humorous quality, Puck incarnates the farcical. Of course warm blood is kept out of the four young romantic lovers so that they will merely amuse us in their farcical mishaps. Farce must play with the surface of things; lovers painted in rich oils would never seem plausible victims of Puck's magical juice in the fairy forest. Now and then there is a flash of depth and power that suggests the tragic realm that lies beyond the comic:

> *Her.* O hell! To choose love by another's eyes!
> *Lys.* Or, if there were a sympathy in choice,
> War, death, or sickness did lay siege to it,
> Making it momentary as a sound,
> Swift as a shadow, short as any dream,
> Brief as the lightning in the collied night,
> That, in a spleen, unfolds both heaven and earth,
> And ere a man hath power to say 'Behold!'

The jaws of darkness do devour it up:
So quick bright things come to confusion.   (I.i.140–149)

And so they do in *Romeo and Juliet,* written about this time. Shadows stand in the wings, so to say, or speak *sotto voce* in all the comedies.

In the next comedy that I review, *The Merchant of Venice,* shadows intrude for many modern readers. But in the *Dream* no discord jars the harmony of farcical, humorous, witty, ironic, and poetic strains. It is Shakespeare's romantic comedy in full flower, unique in introducing the supernatural with finely comic effects. Ironies lack any feeling of intense contradiction; they are kept muted by sportive merriment. All amours are exposed in their radical absurdity but suffered with the amusement of humor. Puck has nothing of the critically comic about him, nothing of the satiric. He sportively creates absurdities even as Theseus recognizes and indulges them. Puck is merely mischievous; he never rebukes or chastises. Tolerance, inseparable from most English humor and almost synonymous with Shakespeare's, permeates the humor of the play, as we see anew if we put it beside *The Comedy of Errors* and *The Taming of the Shrew,* both also long on the farcical, but short on the humorous.

In Shakespeare's playhouse *The Merchant of Venice* was enjoyed as a romantic comedy—villain and all. But the whirligig of time has turned Shylock into a tragic villain for much modern sensibility.[9] Elizabethans did inherit and hold to cruel ways with Jews, but against them our century has perpetrated crimes that paralyze the imagination. No islands entire unto themselves, we are forever conscious of our involvement with the horrible deeds of Hitler and his tribe at Buchenwald and Dachau. Nor, alas, is the shameful story over. Inevitably we look before and after Shylock to the long and disgraceful record of man's inhumanity to a great people. For us, the moving assertion of the Jew's humanity by Shylock slips easily into tragic focus. With difficulty do we take him as the villain in a romantic comedy who happens to be a Jew, though such he assuredly was for Shakespeare's audience. If the tragic can go comic when we are sufficiently detached from it, the comic for one age can turn into the tragic for a later one when detachment is lost amid shifted social and moral settings. The metamorphosis of Shylock the comic villain of yesteryear into the tragic figure that many people find him today shows how truly the comic pivots upon point of view in time.

Yet if we force ourselves to listen to Shylock in his setting without the cries of tortured Jews deafening our ears anew, we recognize in him a variant of a conventional villain in traditional comedy—the miserly old father who stands in the way of the union of young lovers by vainly trying to dam up the onrush of life over and beyond any forms engendered by it. Shylock laments more the loss of his ducats than the loss of his daughter with his jewels to the Christians who promise freedom to her and her lover. Furthermore, the satisfaction aroused by Shylock trumped is that always generated by the old and familiar farcical device of the "trickster tricked." If Gratiano taunts him as a comic butt, his creator dismisses him as one at the end of the fourth act. The humanizing motivations for his villainy were taken in perspective by the Elizabethans. The famous verses that today move us to sympathy with Shylock as almost the symbol of a persecuted people did not ring in their ears long enough to obscure the fact that Shylock was a usurious and alien criminal plotting death for a Venetian citizen. Truth is, those verses that forever motivate and humanize Shylock as a man simply show Shakespeare "understanding the life" (in Santayana's phrase) of his comic villian—the inward seriousness of facts, whatever their outward absurdity.[10] We are free to feel the tragedy of Shylock so long as we do not forget his outward dimension as a comic villain within the framework of a romantic comedy wherein he lives and moves and has his only being.[11]

Shakespeare creates a romantic and comic milieu before he allows us to hear Shylock in significant soliloquy (I.iii.42–53) proclaim his villainy—villainy to be sustained through his dismissal at the end of the fourth act without an echo of him in the last. Bassanio's apostrophe to the Belmont lady of "wondrous virtues" (I.i.161–172) sounds early the note of romantic love that will dominate the play. In the second scene Portia and Nerissa, in chatter freighted with proverbial wisdom, focus on such love in the lively vein of wit and humor that is to mark both as they move the play along, once perspective is kept on Shylock. Portia is the treasure that rewards Bassanio for his wise choice of the casket of lead; she outwits Shylock's murderous design on Antonio; her sportiveness engenders the farcical and ironic ring complications, that hold the finish of the play to the level of romantic comedy. Her puns score points precisely (for example, in V.i.129, 135–137, 244–245) and contrast with Launcelot Gobbo's stumbling upon the wrong word repeatedly to become one of Mrs. Malaprop's many ancestors. This "wit-snapper's" badinage with Jessica (III.v) illustrates how in Elizabethan drama "every fool can play upon the word" (III.v.48); the exuberance of the times frequently overflowed in comic sportiveness with the language. Notable is the way all three casket choosings are taken with a sense of humor by the romantic ladies; thus closely are the romantic and the comic interwoven in the play.

Repetition beyond any pun's footing in it appears and reappears in this play even as it subserves comic effects in the plays already reviewed. The comic impact of repetition lies, perhaps, in the way in which it underscores an absurd contrast between fact and encrusting form.[12] Nerissa repeats Portia step for step in the ring fooling, echoes her speeches from time to time as she doubles the trick on Gratiano. Repetition appears in the taunting of Shylock with his "second Daniel" speeches, of course taken comically by an audience that accepted Shylock as a trickster villain justly caught in his own trap. The repetitious formality of the ring phrase in V.i.193–208 is a pretty illustration of the comic in repeated word play. Repetition figures comically in the multiplied disguises in the play. Gobbo fools his sand-blind father even by giving him the hair of the back of his head (according to an old stage tradition) as his beard. The disguise of Portia and Nerissa as Balthasar and his clerk—a radically comic device—is bedrock for the trial scene and the entire ring episode with its ironies, comic because taken playfully, that emerge in various speeches in the last act—for example, in Gratiano's about his ring:

> I gave it to a youth,
> A kind of boy, a little scrubbed boy,
> No higher than myself, the judge's clerk.   (V.i.161–163)

Jessica's disguise as a boy in eloping with Lorenzo repeats a device always rich in comic potentiality, here involved in a romantic episode, and so used in *The Two Gentlemen*. It is destined for its finest exploitation, of course, in *As You Like It* and *Twelfth Night*. Irony runs hand in hand with such disguise; witness pre-eminently Rosalind and Viola in their love tangles.

The exalting romantic love that pervades the play is the lyricism of many amorous speeches, at its peak in the dialogue of the opening of the last act when Lorenzo and Jessica use an old lyric form to vie with each other in paying tribute to the loveliness of the night—such a night as Troilus, Thisbe, Dido, and Medea hallowed long ago for all true lovers. Our memory of ugly Shylock fades before the beauty of these speeches. The apostrophe to the night even echoes in Portia's "blessed candles of the night" (V.i.220), but not until the intense lyricism overflows into music that accompanies Lorenzo as he speaks his familiar verses about its "sweet power." Music and song appear climactically in the romantic comedies not only to characterize but also to translate the situations that occasion them into the realm of harmonious sound in which comic conflicts and all others can be resolved.[13] An instance is music's sounding when Bassanio is making his tense choice of the leaden casket to the accompaniment of "Tell me, where is fancy bred."[14]

Meeting *The Merchant of Venice* immediately after *A Midsummer Night's Dream*, with its superfine harmony of all strains, invites an appraisal of both as romantic comedies. Both open with romantic lovers in grave difficulties that are eventually resolved happily with all lovers properly paired. In both, the entire last act turns upon the farcical—burlesque of high heroic lovers in the one and trickery of romantic lovers by their playful ladies in the other. And in both, ridiculous clownage amuses us in the middle of complications, though Gobbo and his father are feeble fools beside Bottom and his fellows. Thanks to Puck, all in the *Dream* falls out "preposterously." Apart from the Gobbos, little falls out so in *The Merchant* until the last act after Shylock has been ejected from the love story—though he does have his radically comic dimension as a villainous "trickster tricked" if we keep a right view on him. Yet his ejection is not at all that of a satiric butt. Romantic love again animates pairs of lovers and envelops a play compacted of romantic adventures; such love is shifted into a minor key of devoted friendship in Antonio's loyalty to Bassanio. The caskets are the stuff of stock romance; so, too, is Portia's disguise as a learned doctor to rescue her lover and his friend. But no finely sustained tissue of the poetry of nature subtly unifies all in *The Merchant* as it does in the *Dream;* nor do song and dance crown the last act of *The Merchant*, although music plays a passing role and Lorenzo speaks a classic tribute to its power. Again diverse materials are fused; but the scene of Bassanio's successful choice of a casket, stemming originally from the Orient and having nothing to do with the choice of a wife, seems protrusive beside the felicitous balance of everything in the *Dream*. However, that romantic scene is skilfully made the nexus of all four story interests: in it Bassanio wins Portia and learns that Antonio must forfeit his life to Shylock as the price of his generosity, Jessica and Lorenzo in bringing this sad news link their romance with the central one, and the exchange of rings by the chief romantic lovers prepares for the ironical and farcical perplexities of the last act.[15] Still, the four romantic interests are not kept in such true equipoise as are the four strains in the *Dream*—Theseus and Hippolyta, the farcically confused lovers, the exquisite fairies, and the bumptious rustics enacting "Pyramus and Thisbe." The comic and some of its kin merge well enough with romance, poetry, and music—until we ponder Shylock in our studies and get him out of focus with his setting. He does bring a romantic lover closer to untimely death than any comes in the *Dream*; and Portia's legal point for effecting a rescue seems a *deus ex machina* compared with Puck's handling of love tangles. But Shylock, dropped at the end of the fourth act without having attained the stature of a truly tragic figure, is allowed to cast no shadow over the comic complications of the romantic in the last act. The proportioning of interests in the play proves that its impact is intended to be comic and romantic. Surely we should take Shylock as a somewhat protrusive villain in a romantic comedy inasmuch as just outside our playhouse is world enough in which to face actual Jewish martyrs.

Much Ado About Nothing dramatizes an old story adapted from Bandello, translated by Belleforest, and available in other forms in Ariosto and Spenser. Its romantic kernel is a lover tricked into believing that his betrothed is false by beholding a suitor at her chamber window. Mature adaptation and fine invention turn a story short on probability and certainly not comic into a play most delightfully that. Action that had spread over a year or more is tele-scoped into nine days, four of which are blank. We get the illusion of short time such as the comic operates in. An atmosphere of buoyant life and wit is at once created. Military victory sharpens the air; life will now bound along merrily, we feel, free of death and destruction; and the comic thrives on life unconfined. Victorious Don Pedro is a gay bachelor whose dominant interest at once appears to be matchmaking, a pastime promising fun. The two matches that he undertakes make the main interests of the play and are expertly interlinked: that of Hero and Claudio with its sensational complications is its romantic base; that of Beatrice and Benedick with its superb wit, humor, and irony is its brilliant superstructure—romantic with a difference. Ridiculous Dogberry and his aides farci-cally tie together and ironically resolve the entangle-ments.[16]

Early in the first scene Beatrice launches her "merry war" on Benedick and a "skirmish of wit" in flashing ripostes has the one capping the other to a draw. When his "dear Lady Disdain" has withdrawn and Benedick wittily boasts that his bachelor freedom will never yield to the marriage yoke, Don Pedro cries with the voice of a comic nemesis: "Nay, if Cupid have not spent all his quiver in Venice, thou wilt quake for this shortly" (I.i.273–274). Wit and irony are quickly allied for comic effects; we half expect Don Pedro's Herculean labor of bringing Benedick and Beatrice "into a mountain of affection th' one with th' other" (II.i.382–383). At the outset of the next act Beatrice with rippling wit boasts of her independence of any masculine "piece of valiant dust," mere "clod of wayward marl." The wit in such utterly apt phrases comi-cally reduces Benedick to stature. And the comic repetitive-ness of their boasting foreshadows the inevitable hum-bling of both boasters even as it gives them another comic dimension. When Beatrice at the masked ball abuses Benedick to his face as the "prince's jester, a very dull fool," he ironically calls down retribution upon his head: "If her breath were as terrible as her terminations, there were no living near her; she would infect to the North Star. I would not marry her though she were endowed with all that Adam had left him before he transgress'd" (II.i.256–261). He retreats when "Lady Tongue" engages Don Pedro and Claudio in equally witty dialogue, vaunts her freedom from any mere man, and then withdraws to make way for the setting of the trap that will catch both her and Benedick. When he swallows the bait instantly, the irony is sharpened by his having just scorned Claudio for such a capitulation and by his having just asserted in superbly witty soliloquy his independence of any lady:

> I do much wonder that one man, seeing how much another man is a fool when he dedicates his behaviours to love, will, after he hath laugh'd at such shallow follies in others, become the argument of his own scorn by falling in love; and such a man is Claudio.... May I be so converted and see with these eyes? I cannot tell; I think not. I will not be sworn but love may transform me to an oyster; but I'll take my oath on it, till he have made an oyster of me he shall never make me such a fool. One woman is fair, yet I am well; another is wise, yet I am well; another virtuous, yet I am well; but till all graces be in one woman, one woman shall not come in my grace. Rich she shall be, that's certain; wise, or I'll none; virtuous, or I'll never cheapen her; fair, or I'll never look on her; mild, or come not near me; noble, or not I for an angel; of good discourse, an excellent musician, and her hair shall be of what colour it please God. (II.iii.7–37)

Could wit and irony coalesce more delightfully for comic effect? Warm humor pulses in the concession about the hair of his perfect lady with which he caps his demands on Cupid even as it does in the candor of "I cannot tell" in answer to "May I be converted and see with these eyes?"

Don Pedro, Leonato, Claudio, and Balthasar introduce

sweet music that Benedick with his acute sense (itself
ironic) of the comic clash between fact and romantic fancy
mocks as food for love: "Is it not strange that sheep's
guts should hale souls out of men's bodies?" (II.iii.61–62).
The charming song about men as "deceivers ever" reflects
the theme of their inconstancy with an irony lost on
Benedick, shortly false to his vow to keep to single blessed-
ness. And that irony is multiplied when, the bait in his
mouth, he cries: "I should think this a gull but that the
white-bearded fellow speaks it. Knavery cannot, sure,
hide himself in such reverence" (II.iii.123–125). When the
three tricksters have drawn the net tightly around
Benedick, they cast a like one for Beatrice; Benedick
advances from his hiding place to cry ironically "This
can be no trick," and to justify his capitulation in a soliloquy that reveals both his comical self-assurance and his
humorous humility in his new role as a lover.

> I did never think to marry. I must not seem proud. Happy
> are they that can hear their detractions and can put them
> to mending. They say the lady is fair—'tis a truth, I can bear
> them witness; and virtuous—'tis so, I cannot reprove it; and
> wise, but for loving me—by my troth, it is no addition to her
> wit, nor no great argument of her folly, for I will be horribly in
> love with her. I may chance have some odd quirks and rem-
> nants of wit broken on me because I have railed so long against
> marriage. But doth not the appetite alter? A man loves the meat
> in his youth that he cannot endure in his age. Shall quips and
> sentences and these paper bullets of the brain awe a man
> from the career of his humour? No, the world must be peopled.
> When I said I would die a bachelor, I did not think I should
> live till I were married.   (II.iii.240–253).

Has the voice of humor ever been more delightfully audible in witty prose? Comic correction of male egotism
mingles with amused and humorous humility before shifting facts—ironically not what they appear to Benedick.
In perfectly chosen words Benedick recognizes appetite
altering with time, and also the inability of taunting wit,
mere "paper bullets of the brain," to "awe a man from

the career of his humour" in a "world [that] must be peopled." Like every true humorist, Benedick accepts the rule of changing impulse over form and convention, takes good-naturedly any collision between them, and readily laughs at himself in shifting to a new convention. Ironically again, he already spies "some marks of love" in Beatrice largely because he now has so many in himself, though as yet there are actually none in her; thus subtly does comic irony enfold them both. Marks of that newborn love in Benedick must amaze Beatrice as she disdainfully summons him to dinner and must abide (ironically) in her memory as fertile ground for her immediate baiting by Hero and Ursula. Their comic repetition of the trick is kept from monotony by nice variations in the second playing of it. Comic repetition with a difference comes also in the raillery when Beatrice quickly accepts her new role without any fear of ridicule (even as Benedick had done), and Margaret wittily prescribes "carduus benedictus" for her "cold in the head" even as Benedick's friends treat his "toothache." True humor is in the way all take playfully fresh facts that clash with passing forms.

Raillery aimed at Beatrice does not follow similar shots at Benedick until Don John makes his accusation against Hero, and Dogberry's men straightway arrest Borachio and Conrade; so nicely is this fresh and vital comic line threaded into the movement of the two matches. As many critics have noted, it is fine comic artistry to introduce this frustration of the plot by farcical folk before its high pitch in the church scene, and so leave us free to enjoy the fun of the exposé because we know a happy ending is assured. Depth involvements must always be muted in the development of a comedy.

Dogberry, Verges, and the Watch are mature comic creations—caricatures transformed by artistry into characters, as Kittredge observes.[17] Dogberry's preposterous way with the language, his most arresting earmark, shows the farcical extended with a vengeance into the world of words: those that we actually hear are radically and playfully at odds with those that we expect. A "dogberryism" might be described as a variety of malapropism in which a word is so misused that its sound does not even suggest the intended word ("everlasting redemption" in IV.ii.59 for "everlasting salvation," or "plaintiffs" for "defendants" in V.i.261). The used word is the opposite in sense from that intended, and sense comes through the context that leads us to substitute the right word expected for the wrong one heard. Not that Dogberry is not a master of malapropisms pure and undefiled ("reformed" for "informed" in V.i.262). If we ask wherein all such miscarrying words differ from words used ironically, we may perhaps answer that the like of "tolerable, and not to be endured" arises from sheer ignorance of words on the part of the speaker, who does not mean just what he literally says, though we extract his intent from the context and our own word-hoard—whereas "honest Iago" means for the speaker just what it literally denotes while we, acquainted with facts concealed from him, get a meaning lost to him in his ignorance of them. The linguistic weeds that grow apace in Dogberry's head rebuke the notion that words are ever ultimately more than conventional signs for unfathomable things, unknown and unknowable in themselves—signs "tolerable, and not to be endured" in all the exigencies of life.

The comic chatter of Dogberry and his associates extends beyond any sort of malapropisms to the utterly illogical line in his speech about Borachio and Conrade in V.i.218–224 and in the metamorphosis of Borachio's "deformed thief this fashion is" into a creature "Deformed" who "has been a vile thief this seven year" (III.iii.135). Comic absurdity could hardly go farther in the farcical spinning of falsity from fact. Verges, that shadow of Dogberry that increases his solidity, bungles the language in addressing Leonato (III.v.32–35). In his futile efforts to escape from the magisterial pomposity of his boss, he plays a sort of *zanni* to him. That this ass Dogberry should cry and cry to be so writ down is a consummate stroke in his delineation. It crowns his mayhem on words. The comic irony of his cry recalls ass-headed Bottom; they are also brothers in having a certain modicum of "ass" sense that enables them to stumble through wherever they find themselves. "If you meet a thief, you may suspect him, by virtue of your office, to be no true man; and for such kind of men, the less you meddle or make with them, why, the more is for your honesty" (II.iii.53–56). Dogberry is comically illogical about the thief; yet eventually Borachio can tell the sophisticates: "What your wisdoms could not discover, these shallow fools have brought to light" (V.i.239–240). With multiplied comic irony, the merry plotters when trapping Benedick and Beatrice are being themselves tricked by Don John and his cronies, the while those villains are themselves being outwitted by nitwits.

One trick yields to another in preparing for the finale, but not before Beatrice's challenge to Benedick to prove his love by killing Claudio reminds us how suddenly a comic tone can be dissipated by a sharply tragic note. The accepted challenge tightly links the two matches; then the tragic tension yields to delightfully affectionate dialogue between the lovers in which the old wit still shines but now without heat; the audience knows the villains are caught. If Beatrice gets the better of Benedick in repartee, he cares not. Love, a near neighbor to humor, now makes both playfully affectionate in their fencing:

> *Bene*. . . . And I pray thee now tell me, for which of my bad parts didst thou first fall in love with me?
> *Beat*. For them all together, which maintain'd so politic a state of evil that they will not admit any good part to intermingle with them. But for which of my good parts did you first suffer love for me?   (V.ii.60–66)

The charming naturalness of the questions anchors the

witty banter wherein true humor keeps the peace between shifting facts and accrued conventions.

After Hero has been restored to Claudio in the final scene of the play, this happy reconciliation of sharp wit and tolerant humor marks the encounters between Beatrice and Benedick. They laugh off their halting love sonnets with which Hero and Claudio would embarrass them:

> *Bene.* A miracle! Here's our own hands against our hearts.
> Come, I will have thee; but, by this light, I take thee for pity.
> *Beat.* I would not deny you; but, by this good day, I yield
> upon great persuasion, and partly to save your life, for I was
> told you were in a consumption.
> *Bene.* Peace! I will stop your mouth.
>
> [*Kisses her.*] (V.iv.91–98)

That kiss throws the argument, long tossed to and fro in a sort of comic stichomythia, into the flux of natural impulse to which all that arises from it must finally defer—the flux of facts that the comic forever abruptly points toward. Benedick, swimming in that sea with the strength of true humor, is impervious to mocking wit, mere "paper bullets of the brain":

> *Pedro.* How dost thou, Benedick, the married man?
> *Bene.* I'll tell thee what, Prince: a college of wit-crackers
> cannot flout me out of my humour. Dost thou think I care
> for a satire or an epigram? No. If a man will be beaten with
> brains, 'a shall wear nothing handsome about him. In brief,
> since I do purpose to marry, I will think nothing to any pur-
> pose that the world can say against it; and therefore never
> flout at me for what I have said against it; for man is a giddy
> thing, and this is my conclusion. (V.iv.99–111)

Benedick's "conclusion" on man is just around the corner from Puck's on mortals and close to their creator's comic vision of the fools that all of us mortals be—particularly when in love. Fittingly indeed does Benedick cry to end the play: "Let's have a dance ere we are married," and "Strike up, pipers!" (V.iv.119, 130). The "giddy things" have already been gyrating amorously in much ado about nothing; they slip easily into the dance. That art radically immerses man in the free flux of animal life as does no other; hence a dance most properly ends a comedy. And Benedick rightly calls upon Don Pedro not to think on the apprehended villain until tomorrow; the free comic spirit takes no thought of the morrow.

And, unless in some way modified, it looks to the extant moment with merriment. *Much Ado* stands with *A Midsummer Night's Dream* in being pervaded by a sense of sportive merriment. Puck best incarnates it in the one, Beatrice in the other. The shift from the cool tone of the earlier comedy, for all its beautiful nature imagery, to the warmth of the later is suggested when we turn from the one character to the other. Puck is a supernatural creature, the "pert and nimble spirit of mirth" incarnate, delighted to have all things "befall prepost'rously." Beatrice is warm and vibrant in her "spirit of mirth." Hers is a "merry heart" that "keeps on the windy side of care"; "to be merry best becomes" her; she was "born in a merry hour" to "speak all mirth and no matter"; and "a star dance'd" at her nativity. Hero reports that "she hath often dreamt of unhappiness and wak'd herself with laughing" (II.i.322–361). Humor humanizes her merriment before things that "befall prepost'rously" (what is radically comic) more than it does that of anyone in the *Dream*. Her buoyant spirits are reflected by other leading characters. Sportive Don Pedro declares that Benedick "is all mirth" (III.ii.10). If Don Pedro marks a "contemptible" or scornful spirit in him, he does so in the course of baiting him (II.iii.188); we feel no venom in the satiric touch in his wit; nor do we in Beatrice's scintillating wit. The dazzling wit in both is increasingly mingled with humor as the play advances and they move toward each other. In Benedick's great soliloquies his wit turns readily in upon himself, the while it keeps its keen edge. Margaret has some of Beatrice's high spirits in a more earthy key. She, too, is a wit; Benedick declares that her "wit is as quick as the greyhound's mouth—it catches" (V.ii.11). When she playfully lectures Beatrice in laying "carduus benedictus" to her heart, she speaks with the voice of natural instinct, puncturing Beatrice's feigned ignorance of the point and her pretense not to be looking for a husband as other women do. Margaret's blunt cry that Hero's heart shall shortly be heavier "by the weight of a man" attests the animal base of comic wit just before the play rises to a grave plane. Even the mad lack of expert "verbal marksmanship" in Dogberry's diction but throws into relief the happy alliance elsewhere of brilliant wit with humor and farcical tricks. A neat minor moment that illustrates the pervasive sportiveness in the humor of the play comes when Don Pedro replies illogically to Dogberry to keep step with that creature's lack of logic (V.i.225–234) and indulge him as "this learned constable."

The comic base of *Much Ado* is the farcical tricks that catapult Benedick and Beatrice into love and the disclosure by "shallow fools" of villainy to which the wits were blind. Benedick is the object of corrective comedy much as Berowne and his associates are in their vows to live without ladies; so, too, Beatrice in vowing to live independently of any mere man. But warm humor permeates them as it does no one equally in *Love's Labour's Lost*. Beatrice is a cousin far removed by her wit and humor from termagant Katherina, tamed by slapstick techniques. The radically comic tricks and turns in *Much Ado* rise on the wings of superlative wit into humorous characterization expressed in ironic action that ranges from the doings of Benedick and Beatrice down to those of Dogberry. No truly satiric notes are heard. Music aids, and a dance suitably crowns all.

C. T. Prouty has shown that in the Hero-Claudio story there is a downgrading of romantic figures as compared with their prototypes in the sources.[18] Beatrice and Benedick, from the outset rebels against idealizing romantic love, end in a sane love shorn of romantic excesses.

In *Much Ado* the comic integrates with the romantic by deflating its excesses through wit and humor and radically comic tricks.

No one has ever mistaken Don John for a tragic villain in a romantic comedy. Although he and his henchmen do bring the Hero-Claudio story to the brink of disaster even as Shylock does the romantic love story in *The Merchant*, no sooner has Hero been falsely accused than those villains are apprehended by Dogberry and his Watch. The countering of villainy comes, not by a nice legal point made by a romantic heroine disguised as a learned clerk, but by farcical illiterates. They and the tricks played on Benedick and Beatrice give the play a radically comic base not matched in *The Merchant*. The radically comic and the humorous modify romantic love as they do not in the earlier play. Fresh harmonies are just ahead in *As You Like It* and *Twelfth Night*.

In *As You Like It* Shakespeare follows closely the story of Thomas Lodge's charming pastoral romance *Rosalynde*. He tones down the violence of the struggle between Saladyne (his Oliver) and Rosader (Orlando) at the outset of the novel. The love story of Rosader and Rosalynde, made home base for the comic spirit in the play, is handled in such high romantic fashion in the novel that only Coridon (Corin) is at all humorous. But the romantic heroines of the play, Rosalind and Celia, are infused with wit and humor; and the free creations—Le Beau, Jaques, Touchstone, Audrey, William, and Sir Oliver Martext—are rich in comic facets. The romantic plot of the play yields in interest to comic character and situation expressed in witty dialogue. We may well attend to the folk who speak it. Once the ambling story is under way, strains of the radically comic, the critically comic, the humorous, the ironic, the witty, and the satiric intricately fuse; music and sweet poetry agree and all yield to dance at the finish.

In the slow-paced opening, Orlando appears as a hero of traditional romance in Elizabethan dress, denied his rightful inheritance by his envious elder brother. Soon he fells a wrestler engaged by that brother to destroy him, then falls in love at first sight with the banished Duke's daughter—who at once loves him. But just before that enamorment, Rosalind and Celia, the usurping duke's daughter and her devoted friend, catch the comic pitch of the play when they resolve to seek mirth in adversity, to find sport in love, and to use the wit nature gave them "to flout at Fortune." Such an intent is essentially that of the mature comic spirit in Shakespeare's romantic comedies.

> *Cel.* ... my sweet Rose, my dear Rose, be merry.
>
> *Ros.* From henceforth I will, coz, and devise sports. Let me see. What think you of falling in love?
>
> *Cel.* Marry, I prithee do, to make sport withal! But love no man in good earnest, nor no further in sport neither than with safety of a pure blush thou mayst in honour come off again.
>
> *Ros.* What shall be our sport then?
>
> *Cel.* Let us sit and mock the good housewife Fortune from her wheel, that her gifts may henceforth be bestowed equally.   (I.ii.25–36)

Those speeches have the maturely comic stance toward life that I at the outset sought to describe in defining the sense of humor in a man who, having looked before and after, yet knows how to live wisely and well in the extant moment.

Fortune (or Shakespeare's artistry) now sends Touchstone, that master "whetstone of the wits," to trump the witty ladies on fortune versus nature with expert foolery. He juggles a knight without honor, non-existent beards on the chins of the ladies, mustard, and pancakes in asserting the right of fools to "speak wisely what wise men do foolishly." Soon the wit of the three overwhelms the elegant Le Beau, amusingly short on a sense of humor. He heralds Charles, the usurping duke's wrestler, now challenged by Orlando. In the style of an Elizabethan gentleman who has read his *Euphues* and the sonneteers, Orlando pays his devotions to the two ladies before over-throwing Charles—and the heart of "heavenly Rosalind." When she, pensive about her lost father and her new love, laments "O, how full of briers is this working-day world!" Celia answers with the wisdom of the comic spirit: "They are but burrs, cousin, thrown upon thee in holiday foolery. If we walk not in the trodden paths, our very petticoats will catch them." The dialogue just here is finely illustrative of the fusion of wit and humor:

> *Ros.* I could shake them off my coat. These burrs are in my heart.
> *Cel.* Hem them away.
> *Ros.* I would try, if I could cry 'hem!' and have him.
> *Cel.* Come, come, wrestle with thy affections.
> *Ros.* O, they take the part of a better wrestler than myself!
> *Cel.* O, a good wish upon you! You will try in time, in despite of a fall.   (I.iii.16–25)

Rosalind's pun is in key. Celia's voice is that of the comic spirit, wise with wit and humor as I have explicated those terms. Even when Celia turns "these jests out of service" to "talk in good earnest" about the tangles of briars and burrs in this "working-day" world (as all of us needs must between our free moments in the tangle of living), wit and the wisdom of humor do not desert her. So sustained, the true friends face together the banishment that is straightway imposed upon Rosalind by Duke Frederick. Rosalind disguised as Ganymede and Celia as "his" sister Aliena, and both fittingly accompanied by the jester Touchstone, will seek the true duke exiled in the Forest of Arden. Celia cries: "Now go we in content / To liberty, and not to banishment" (I.iii.139–140).

The banished Duke opens the next act by moralizing his lot in Arden in verses that mingle sense and senti-ment. But in being irked by the goring of "poor dap-pled fools" for venison and grieving for the "hairy fool" that "stood on th' extremest verge of the swift brook,

/ Augmenting it with tears,"[19] he is ironically more brother than he knows to sentimental Jaques in his grief for that stricken stag, down whose "innocent nose" the "big round tears" coursed "in piteous chase." Both men invite the smile of the correctively comic as they let sentiment run away with sense. Doubly does Jaques do so when he moves on from "weeping and commenting / Upon the sobbing deer," "left and abandoned of his velvet friends," to

> swearing that we
> Are mere usurpers, tyrants, and what's worse,
> To fright the animals and to kill them up
> In their assign'd and native dwelling place.   (II.i.60–63)

But more of Jaques anon.

When the exiles, weary in spirits, reach idyllic Arden, witty Touchstone is the very voice of animal actuality that hugs mother earth in comic contrast with anything beyond it:

> *Touch.* I care not for my spirits if my legs were not weary.
>   . . .
> *Cel.* I pray you bear with me; I cannot go no further.
> *Touch.* For my part, I had rather bear with you than bear you. Yet I should bear no cross if I did bear you, for I think you have no money in your purse.
> *Ros.* Well, this is the Forest of Arden.
> *Touch.* Ay, now am I in Arden, the more fool I! When I was at home, I was in a better place; but travellers must be content.   (II.iv.2–18)

With nice irony the fool of dauntless wit shames the philosophical ladies in actually practicing their comic code of keeping mirthful in adversity by flouting fickle fortune.

Now the exiles hear the young shepherd Silvius lament to the old shepherd Corin his unrequited love for Phebe. Silvius is comically confident of the uniqueness of his love sighs, particularly in three times telling Corin "Thou has't not lov'd" if "thou remayb'rest not the slightest folly / That ever love did make thee run into" (II.iv.33–35).

When sympathetic Rosalind cries, "Alas, poor shepherd! Searching of thy wound, / I have by hard adventure found mine own" (II.iv.42–43), Touchstone undercuts their romantic flights with an account of his wooing of dairy-maid Jane Smile, aided by batlet and peascod. There is genial mockery and comic truth in his conclusion: "We that are true lovers run into strange capers; but as all is mortal in nature, so is all nature in love mortal in folly" (II.iv.53–56).[20] The comic is a great democrat: if it looks to life and life more abundantly here and now, for the fun within life rather than to our being in death in the midst of life, it is like death a great leveler.

Was comedy's love of life in the moment ever more happily reflected than in "Under the Greenwood Tree" that Amiens now sings? He knows that sweet music will make Monsieur Jaques melancholy, that that gentleman, "wrapped in a most humorous sadness," will inevitably, as he himself confesses, "suck melancholy out of a song as a weasel sucks eggs." Shortly the Duke, learning that melancholy Jaques has just been "merry, hearing of a song," cries:

If he, compact of jars, grow musical,
We shall have shortly discord in the spheres.
Go seek him; tell him I would speak with him.   (II.vii.5–7)

Soon Jaques is reporting how his "lungs began to crow like chanticleer" upon his hearing the motley fool Touchstone "moral on the time" in which men "ripe and rot." Jaques longs for a motley coat—yet not for the fun and joy of wearing it:

Invest me in my motley. Give me leave
To speak my mind, and I will through and through
Cleanse the foul body of th' infected world,
If they will patiently receive my medicine.   (II.vii.58–61)

The voice sounds not like that of a humorist, but like that of the traditional satirist, audible in much drama about the time *As You Like It* was written. But is Jaques a true satirist? Is he a railing malcontent of vintage 1600? There has been much argument about it. The Duke counters:

Most mischievous foul sin, in chiding sin.
For thou thyself hast been a libertine,
As sensual as the brutish sting itself;
And all th' embossed sores and headed evils
That thou with license of free foot has caught,
Wouldst thou disgorge into the general world. (II.vii.64–69)

Jaques's defense has been neatly paraphrased, in summary:" If my satire fits any individual, it will certainly not corrupt him. If it does not fit him, no harm will be done."[21] Kittredge has also reminded us that we are not to think of Jaques as a libertine in the specialized sense of the word in modern English, "as a worn-out and disgusted roué."[22] Rosalind with her fine sense of humor takes accurate measure of Jaques, as we shall shortly see. In forever moralizing the spectacle he fails to get its free comic dimension, to laugh heartily at its utter absurdity in its momentary contrast with the flux beneath it. His true home is not in the world as a laughing philosopher or as a genuine satirist, but out of it in a life of disillusioned retirement to which he appropriately withdraws at the finish of the play: "I am for other than for dancing measures" (V.iv.199). Not a kill-joy like Malvolio, he is a "lack-joy," if one may coin the epithet. He does amuse others and is mildly amused in his sentimental fashion. He is certainly food for the critically comic, possibly for the satiric, however much he may himself wish to "cleanse the foul body of th' infected world." "Wrapped in a most humorous sadness," he misses the merriment of life. His most famous speech, potent in its images that evoke the "seven ages" of our "strange eventful history," is a very "lack-joy" performance that looks over life for the sad truth of it, not directly at it for the free fun in it. The song that succeeds the speech quite transcends its vision: in spite of the winter wind's being not so unkind as man's ingratitude, in spite of most friendship's being feigning and most loving mere folly, in spite of the freezing bitter sky "that dost not bite so nigh / As benefits forgot" and sting "so sharp / As friend rememb'red not"—our refrain is "heigh-ho, unto the green holly!" that age-old symbol of mirth; for "this life is most jolly" if we can but hold to the freely comic slant on it within the extant moment.

Except for its brief first scene, Act III is given over to amorous tangles in the Forest of Arden, all presented from the comic angle in persistently witty dialogue in which puns abound. Pastoralism that romanticizes love and idealizes rustic life comes in for the mild rebuke of the correctively comic—or the gently satiric?—that yet always defers to humor. The sense of relativity that is bedrock for humor is nicely shown by old Corin in wit combat with Touchstone that pits the merits of the town against those of the country: "Those that are good manners at the court are as ridiculous in the country as the behaviour of the country is most mockable at the court" (III.ii.46–49). Touchstone's town wit does outsmart the simple old shepherd: Corin defers to "too courtly a wit for me" with "I'll rest." Yet we feel that he rests where good sense well might:

> Sir, I am a true labourer; I earn that I eat, get that I wear; owe no man hate, envy no man's happiness; glad of other men's good, content with my harm; and the greatest of my pride is to see my ewes graze and my lambs suck.
>
> (III.ii.77– 81)

Corin's "content" recalls Chaucer's "hertes suffisaunce" that blessed the "povre wydwe" of the Nun's Priest's Tale. What if Touchstone worries Corin with more wit that makes him a sinner in living by the copulation of cattle and playing bawd to a bell-wether? Such a "true labourer" is impervious to Touchstone's shots except insofar as they make for sheer fun. Corin, living close to mother earth after his honest fashion, is no target for the correctively comic.

But the romantic lovers decidedly are. When Ganymede reads Orlando's extravagant verses lauding Rosalind, Touchstone immediately ridicules them with verses that mock their flighty love by allying it with that of harts and hinds and cats. And when Celia comes in with more of the stuff that Orlando is hanging on trees, she subjects Rosalind, who feigns ignorance of their authorship, to a delicious blend of wit and humor wherein the correctively comic darts only prick the skin because the sportiveness of genial humor blunts them. Delightful is Rosalind's demand that her nine quick questions about Orlando be answered "in one word." "You must borrow me Gargantua's mouth first" (III.ii.238) from Celia jerks amorous ardor back to nature's bounds. Orlando, ridiculed as "Signor Love" by "lack-love" Jaques, forces a retreat by that "Monsieur Melancholy"—better to have men foolish in love than foolishly denouncing it, the maturely comic spirit would say. After Rosalind has wittily proved to Orlando that time "travels in divers paces with divers persons," she playfully abuses one who "hangs odes upon hawthorns, and elegies on brambles; all, forsooth, deifying the name of Rosalind" (III.ii.379–381). Her catalogue of the stock lover's symptoms mocks the earmarks of conventional amorousness; and her undertaking to cure Orlando by having him pretend to woo her in the guise of Ganymede refines upon disguise (or mistaken identity) as a comic device that is involved in all the comedies and increasingly pivotal in the development of the romantic ones.

Disguise as a tool of the comic is apparently as old as comedy itself and certainly omnipresent throughout its history. Complex accounts of the psychology of its operation need not hold us. I would simply recognize it as uniquely potent in effecting a comic contrast between surface appearance and basic actuality. Everyone knows how the Elizabethan convention of boy actors in all women's parts gave an underlying "disguise" strain to much acting in Shakespeare's day, how that convention was a standing invitation to the disguise of those "heroines" as young men, and how repeatedly and brilliantly that convention is exploited by Shakespeare from Silvia to Viola. For us today, accustomed to seeing our favorite actresses as Shakespeare's ladies, the comic edge of the plays is sharp when we recall the old convention, in a way it was not for a Globe audience that had known no other. Yet we may be sure that the boy playing the "Rosalind-Ganymede-Rosalind" whom Orlando pretends to woo— actually does woo—bred a pretty lot of ironies and ambiguities for that audience.[23] Only Viola exploits the device to a finer pitch than Rosalind reaches when Orlando woos her as Ganymede playing Rosalind, while Phebe falls in love with that Ganymede.

Good nature permeates all of Rosalind's persistent wit. Because she is even "humorously conscious of her own sentimentality,"[24] she sheds ridicule as Orlando, the Duke, and Jaques, dull-eyed about their own absurdities, do not. When Celia teases her about Orlando, Rosalind tosses the flashing ball of wit to and fro with gay good humor and a sense of the absurdity in everything, herself included. Phebe's capitulation to her Ganymede breeds dialogue rich in comic irony. Rosalind is tart, yet lightly so, about Phebe's harshness to her fawning swain, then penetratingly critical of Jaques because she, unlike him and like all the major comic heroines in Shakespeare, has the invincibility given by true humor. In egotistically claiming his melancholy as "mine own, compounded of many simples, extracted from many objects, and indeed the sundry contemplation of my travels, in which my often rumination wraps me in a most humorous sadness" (IV.i.16–20),[25] Jaques invites the just rebuke of the correctively comic that Rosalind gives him: "And your experience makes you sad. I had rather have a fool to make me merry than experience to make me sad—and to travel for it too!" (IV.i.27–29). Her ridicule of him as the exemplar of many Elizabethan gentlemen who lost their common sense in their Continental travels is tinged with humor that keeps it from the hot rebuke which the satirists of the times regularly gave such men; witness her amused "and to travel for it too!" She does not lash him; she laughs at him. The "love-prate" in which Rosalind indulges as she gives Orlando his amorous education in the pretended wooing of Ganymede shows constantly an acute sense of the comic contrast between fact and fancy: "Men have died from time to time, and worms have eaten them, but not for love" (IV.i.107–108). In passing she topples Troilus and Leander from their high romantic pedestals. The tissue of wit and irony that Rosalind and Orlando spin is a delightfully comic ridiculing of the absurd postures of romantic lovers. Worth underscoring is the sheer playfulness in all this comic fooling. Celia brings all anew into comic focus with her conclusive "And I'll sleep," in blunt animal contrast with Rosalind's love prattle climaxed by "I'll tell thee, Aliena, I cannot be out of sight of Orlando. I'll go find a shadow, and sigh till he come" (IV.i.221–224). Rosalind's humorous playfulness in love appears anew in her dubbing Phebe's amorous verses to Ganymede "railing"—to the abashment of Silvius. With "Alas, poor shepherd!" Celia gives a warmly human dimension to conventional Silvius, subjected to Rosalind's tongue-in-cheek abuse as a doting lover—the while she dotes on Orlando. Repeatedly Celia is a realistic foil for Rosalind.

Hard on the heels of these sophisticated lovers come Touchstone and his Audrey for a jolly burlesque of all their romancing. When Audrey proudly asserts that she is "not a slut," though she thanks the gods she is "foul," we meet such a comic contrast with the ladies as we got when Touchstone introduced his former flame Jane Smile. In his readiness to marry this "poor virgin, sir, an ill-favour'd thing, sir, but mine own" (V.iv.60–61), Touchstone makes ridiculous anew the romantic lovers who fail to recognize their absurdity in hithering and thithering around matrimony. "Monsieur Melancholy," shocked that Touchstone is ready to be "married under a bush like a beggar" by a hedge priest so that "not being well married, it will be a good excuse for me hereafter to leave my wife" (III.iii.94–95), has a "lack-lustre eye" for the sportive spirit toward holy matrimony that Touchstone assumes—perhaps in part to bait that melancholy philosopher.[26] The meshing of the comedy of romance with the country comedy of Touchstone and Audrey getting married is seen in the repetition ceremony in which Orlando "weds" Ganymede playing Rosalind while Celia acts the priest.[27] The serious reporting of Orlando's near-disastrous encounter with a lioness by the repentant and converted Oliver (taken in comic stride with the swooning of Rosalind construed now as counterfeit and now as not) yields at once to Touchstone and Audrey, this time trailed by bumpkin William. He strikes a fresh note in their burlesque variation on the romantic love that is basic in the play. All is handled with humor that suffers the conventions, however much at odds with animal facts.

The ironies and ambiguities of Rosalind in her multiple roles with Orlando, Phebe, Silvius, and even herself come to the brink of comic climax in the repetition of the speeches of the four of them at the end of V.ii. Rosalind, with her unfailing sense of the absurd, comically caps this refrain-like patter when she protests: "Pray you, no more of this; 'tis like the howling of Irish wolves against the moon" (V.ii.118–119). That touch of animal actuality topples the tower of amorous absurdity. In the next scene Touchstone and Audrey, hoping it is "no dishonest desire to desire to be a woman of the world," root romance anew in the earth before "It was a Lover and his Lass" voices perfectly the pastoralism of native cornfields wherein lovers unaffectedly "take the present time"—as do all folk with a true sense of the comedy of existence. Touchstone's mockery of what he calls a "foolish song" with a "very untunable note" is the agile comic spirit itself turning in playful mockery upon whatever has taken form within the flux of passing moments. His foolery is rampant as in the last scene he dazzles the Duke and Jaques with his fun-loving wit, at ease before whatever the lottery of life casts up, be it a courtier's follies or the "lie seven times removed (bear your body more seeming, Audrey)." That parenthesis is a superb flash of Touchstone's quicksilverish sense of comic fact. The poised Duke rather than "Monsieur Melancholy" rightly renders perceptive judgment on Touchstone: "He uses his folly like a stalking horse, and under the presentation of that he shoots his wit" (V.iv.111–112).[28] His "shooting" at anything whatever in mortal folly is the free comic spirit in action. Often Rosalind is that too. Romantic love and pastoralism forgetful of underlying animal facts are fit targets for both of them.

Rosalind, framed happily by a little finale masque presided over by Hymen, gives each lover his sensible due, and the god of wedlock echoes her. His dukedom and his daughter restored to him, the Duke cries: "Play, music, and you brides and bridegrooms all, / With measure heap'd in joy, to th' measures fall" (V.iv.184–185). The comic spirit overflows into song and dance whence it long ago arose. Even "Monsieur Melancholy" gives his "lack-joy" blessings to the lot of lovers, if with a disillusioned word for Touchstone and his Audrey, before rightly withdrawing to the life contemplative.

Humor, irony, the correctively comic, and wit pervade *As You Like It*. Disguise gives it a radically comic base and its most theatrical moment—Ganymede's unmasking to disclose Rosalind. Correctively comic strokes deflate the pretensions of romantic love and pastoralism that have forgotten the facts of earth; but nowhere is there the scorn and derision of virile satire. Humor blunts any satirical intents. Even Jaques is not ejected as a satirical butt at the finish; he just withdraws from the company of jolly folk. Constantly song and lovely poetry fuse with these comic elements to create a realm in which we in our distracted days can "fleet the time carelessly as they did in the golden world"—if somewhat ironically inasmuch as Shakespeare in this play is laughing good-naturedly at the escapism of pastoral drama.

Twelfth Night embraces and harmonizes with unique fulness all the comic strains and most other ones that have appeared in its predecessors. In it the radically comic, the humorous, the satiric, the witty, and the ironic blend with romantic love and adventure, poetry, songs, and dance in a most complex and elaborate pattern. It sustains imponderables of character and atmosphere that of course no analysis can ever fully capture.

The main plot of *Twelfth Night* preserves much of the romantic material of its immediate source, the tale *Of Apolonius and Silla* in *Riche his Farewell to Militarie Profession* (1581). Its core is the separation of a sister from her brother by shipwreck and subsequent disguise and amorous adventures (like Viola's) that breed tangles to be resolved happily at last by the disclosure of her real identity. Rich had made notable changes in his source —the thirty-sixth story in Part II of Matteo Bandello's *Novelle*—and Shakespeare alters Rich's narrative, particularly by interlocking with its romantic adventures the comic doings that are apparently his own invention.[29] He so intimately links the antics of Maria, Sir Toby, Sir Andrew, and Feste with the amusing amours of Orsino, Viola, Olivia, and Sebastian that scrutiny of one group for comic facets compels scrutiny of the other. Everyone stands upon the radically comic, as the denouement clearly reveals.

The farcical cornerstone of an elaborate structure appears when Viola, separated from her twin brother Sebastian by shipwreck, resolves to seek her fortune at Orsino's court disguised as the youth Cesario. As Cesario she propels the main movement of the play through to its finish.

Cesario is in essence a radically comic device, an ultimate evolvement of the various mistaken identities and disguises that have figured in all the comedies, romantic and farcical. A twin sister disguised as a youth now precipitates radically comic situations that surpass in finesse those ranging from the confusions of the doubled male twins in *The Comedy of Errors* to Ganymede in *As You Like It*.

The first comic situation into which Viola's disguise catapults her comes when Orsino commissions her to woo Olivia for him and she confesses:

> I'll do my best
> To woo your lady. [*Aside*] Yet a barful strife!
> Whoe'er I woo, myself would be his wife.   (I.iv.40–42)

Concomitant with its development runs an irony to be repeatedly refined beyond its first emergence in Orsino's lovely speech to the "dear lad" with "Diana's lip" and the "small pipe" that is "as the maiden's organ, shrill and sound" (I.iv.29–33). Next Cesario, unselfishly wooing Olivia for Orsino in superbly witty dialogue, captivates that lady. This superimposed complex of the radically comic, the ironic, the humorous, and the witty is spun fine by Viola's fencing with enamored Olivia in tense stichomythia:

> *Oli.* Stay.
> I prithee tell me what thou think'st of me.
> *Vio.* That you do think you are not what you are.
> *Oli.* If I think so, I think the same of you.
> *Vio.* Then think you right. I am not what I am.
> *Oli.* I would you were as I would have you be!
> *Vio.* Would it be better, madam, than I am?
> I wish it might; for now I am your fool.   (III.i.149–156)

The dialogue gets part of its comic impact from being built on repetition, a fundamentally comic device. But the radically comic in all amorous scenes between Viola and Olivia is pervaded by a winsome charm and tender humor that rises from Viola's character. The complex of this scene takes a new farcical turn when Sir Toby shortly maneuvers cowardly Sir Andrew into challenging Cesario, thought to be deflecting Olivia from that preposterous suitor. Now comes a pyramiding of mistaken identities that interlocks all the leading characters. Antonio mistakes Cesario for Sebastian whom he had befriended after the shipwreck; then Feste, Sir Andrew, and Sir Toby successively mistake Sebastian for Cesario—those two ridiculous knights exchanging blows with Sebastian. Next Olivia mistakes Sebastian for Cesario and happily wins at once him whom she thinks Cesario. Antonio, now arrested as Orsino's enemy, again mistakes Cesario for Sebastian; and Olivia, thinking Cesario is Sebastian, demands the wedlock that the latter has just promised her. The comic bewilderment of Orsino, Olivia, and Cesario is complete when Sir Andrew rushes in with his head cracked by Sebastian whom he had thought to be Cesario, and Sir Toby limps after him with a bloody coxcomb got from the same strong arm. When Sebastian enters and confronts Cesario, Orsino exclaims: "One face, one voice, one habit, and two persons!" (V.i.223). In a final turn the whirligig of time unmasks Viola and makes everybody happy except Malvolio, who has all along mistaken himself for far better than the "affection'd ass" that he is, and now mistakes Feste for a cleric.

The third scene of the play introduces the principals of the underplot in characteristic stances: bibulous Sir Toby, fatuous Sir Andrew, and sensible Maria, vibrant with wit and mischievous fun. Two radically comic interests fuse in this area of the play: the gulling of Malvolio and the fooling of cowardly Sir Andrew into a duel with Cesario. "I am sure care's an enemy to life," cries Sir Toby in his first speech, as if a spokesman for the elemental comic spirit that prevails in the romps he leads. Drink, classic (if treacherous) aide of the comic in fighting that enemy, inspires him chronically. Shortly he and Maria are bombarding with wit that "foolish knight" Sir

Andrew, whom Sir Toby has in profitable tow as a match
for his niece Olivia. This marvelous simpleton's efforts
to keep step with the wit of his betters are as ridiculous
as his spindle legs when shortly they cut capers. Dance,
just an overflowing of life in abundance in the preceding
comedies, is now expressive of comic character too. Sir
Andrew's forlorn vanity and utter obtuseness are so
natural that they remind us that the pathetic is close akin
to the unfeignedly natural, comical because caught in a
world of conventions it never made. Like that fat boy
in Dickens (as Santayana saw him), Sir Andrew would
be impervious to laughter in the least malicious. In carous-
ing with Sir Toby he philosophizes that life "consists of
eating and drinking" even as might the unrefined comic
spirit itself. That ultimate love song "O mistress mine,
where are you roaming?" sung by Feste shows the *carpe
diem* theme perfectly attuned to the "present mirth [that]
hath present laughter" in comedy. The song makes way
for such a caterwauling of catches that even Maria calls
for quiet. Now Malvolio, just heralded by Sir Toby's
ridicule of him as a Peg-a-Ramsey, stalks in to rebuke
the merrymakers in an affectedly "dignified and elegant
style."[30] This kill-joy is exactly appraised by shrewd Maria
when she promises her inspired gulling of him: "The devil
a Puritan that he is, or anything constantly but a time-
pleaser; an affection'd ass, that cons state without book
and utters it by great swarths; the best persuaded of himself; so cramm'd, as he thinks, with excellencies that it is
his grounds of faith that all that look on him love him"
(II.iii.158–165). Such insufferable pretension and self-love
invite the correctively comic or the satiric to fall to. The
trick played on Malvolio, radically comic, breeds amusement; yet its intent is clearly corrective, even satiric. "Shall
this fellow live?" Sir Toby cries for all of us at the height
of Malvolio's preposterous strutting in the glory of a greatness that he ironically fancies thrust upon him. Malvolio's
first words reveal the eternal enemy of the freely comic:

he hotly rebukes lovers of "cakes and ale," of a life of irresponsible fun in the extant moment—all the fun-makers around him. His ill nature even distorts after its own image Olivia's message about the ring; he churlishly delivers it to departing Cesario with falsifying twists. Such a disagreeable and vainglorious "trout" is easily "caught with tickling" by the three merry-makers. Lacking utterly the humility and circumspection of humor ("Ay, an you had any eye behind you, you might see more detraction at your heels than fortunes before you" [II.v.148–150]), Malvolio swiftly struts in blind egotism to his comic down-fall. Irony engulfs him: "I do not now fool myself, to let imagination jade me; for every reason excites to this, that my lady loves me" (II.v.172–173). Actually, "imagination blows him." Pride, that deadliest of the seven deadly sins for medieval moralists, forever makes a man vulnerable to correction by the comic spirit—and overthrow by the tragic. Malvolio's smiling and smiling as he struts, cross-gartered in yellow stockings, that he thinks are to his lady's taste when actually she loathes them, is a master stroke in his comic delineation. He who never relaxes in free laughter at himself or anything else now plasters smiles on his countenance to effect a profitable match with his mistress; these natural signs of a sense of humor before the absurdity of things are ironically used to denote a total lack of one. What Malvolio construes as Jove's doings, we know to be the trick of pranksters operating on "an affection'd ass." The comic irony is involuted again with Fabian's "If this were play'd upon a stage now, I could condemn it as an improbable fiction" (III.iv.140–141). It is and it is not—just that. Sir Toby's "comical parody of a gentle, coaxing style"[31] with the gulled "bawcock" or "chuck" ("Ay, biddy, come with me") evokes: "Go, hang yourselves all! You are idle shallow things; I am not of your element" (III.iv.136–137). Malvolio is exactly right; their "element" is that of the comic; his never is. He is ironically unaware that his "element" of vanity and self-love is that upon which the correctively comic and the satiric thrive. Here they both act upon him jointly—and students understandably argue the proportion of each in the treatment of him.[32] Malvolio's ejection from the happy finale of the play—unregenerate, for his last words are "I'll be reveng'd on the whole pack of you!" (V.i.386)—is the traditional way of the satiric with its butt. Olivia's sympathetic "Alas poor fool, how have they baffled thee!" (V.i.377) and "He hath been most notoriously abus'd" (V.i.387) express the feelings of a sentimental lady—hardly those of Shakespeare and his audience.[33] Feste, "the merriest of all Shakespeare's fools,"[34] incarnates the comic spirit throughout the play and checkmates with his wit the major characters. He taunts Malvolio at its finish with echoes of his most absurd speeches. Yet it is Fabian and the ruling Duke who there set the tolerant temper in which we are to leave the gulling of Malvolio. Fabian asks that Olivia "let no quarrel, nor no brawl to come, / Taint the conditions of this present hour" (V.i.364–365). "In hope it shall not," he most freely confesses that he and Sir Toby and Maria

> Set this device against Malvolio here,
> Upon some stubborn and uncourteous parts
> We had conceiv'd against him.
>   . . .
> How with a sportful malice it was follow'd
> May rather pluck on laughter than revenge,
> If that the injuries be justly weigh'd
> That have on both sides pass'd.   (V.i.368–376)

Concord and laughter should succeed any malice that has been merely sportful; for if one side of "sportful malice" is corrective or satiric, the other is radically comic. The dominant Duke would pursue Malvolio and "entreat him to a peace." And, significantly, Feste ends the comedy by singing that supreme song of reconciliation to life as it is in "this present hour," a fleeting mixture of comic this and tragic that while the "rain it raineth every day." Humor and comic irony agreeing with sweet poetry enfold any corrective intents, any satiric thrusts at Malvolio.

If Malvolio chiefly evokes the satiric and the correctively comic, Orsino and Olivia as sentimental self-deceivers are mildly treated by the latter. Fabian explicates the action of those strains; Feste best expresses the radically comic, the merriment, and the wit in the play. Maria conceives the trick played on Malvolio, and Sir Toby, the tricking of Cesario and Sir Andrew into a duel; but this clown pretending to be the parson Sir Topas is the final lord high executioner of Malvolio. However, in his trumping every major character with his wit, Feste's comic function is seen unalloyed with any satiric one. He will jest wittily with anybody about anything; he out-fences Orsino, Olivia, Viola, and Sebastian. Less the humorist and tool of the correctively comic than Touchstone, he is more the free tool of the radically comic, wittily aware of the absurd dimension of everything. As such he plays agilely with any man-made conventions for sheer amusement in the moment.[35] Has ever wit been more brilliantly turned to the service of the radically comic?

And yet it is not Feste who most gives *Twelfth Night* its unique quality as a romantic comedy. It is Viola. Her mellow wit and humor, her muted and unselfish love. To do more than quote from passages familiar to the reader would be "profanation" to ears in which they have long rung with their own "divinity," "as secret as maiden-head."

> *Vio.* Most radiant, exquisite, and unmatchable beauty—I pray you tell me if this be the lady of the house, for I never saw her. I would be loath to cast away my speech; for, besides that it is excellently well penn'd, I have taken great pains to con it. . . .
> *Oli.* . . .Where lies your text?
> *Vio.* In Orsino's bosom.
> *Oli.* In his bosom? In what chapter of his bosom?

> *Vio.* To answer by the method, in the first of his heart.
> *Oli.* O, I have read it! it is heresy. Have you no more to say?
> *Vio.* Good madam, let me see your face.
> *Oli.* Have you any commission from your lord to negotiate with my face? You are now out of your text. But we will draw the curtain and show you the picture. [*Unveils.*] Look you, sir, such a one I was this present. Is't not well done?
> *Vio.* Excellently done, if God did all.   (I.v.181–186, 240–255)

Wit, paradoxically keen but never cutting because restrained by the sympathy and playfulness of humor, is Viola's constant aide in all her delicate impasses when as Cesario she unselfishly woos Olivia for her master, and Olivia discloses her passion for Cesario. Viola humorously suffers the ironies and distresses that her disguise breeds amid facts absurdly at odds with forms and conventions. She keeps always the relaxed and amused detachment of true humor. She knows that only time that weaves our comic tangles can untie her knot.

> How will this fadge? My master loves her dearly;
> And I (poor monster) fond as much on him;
> And she (mistaken) seems to dote on me.
> What will become of this? As I am a man,
> My state is desperate for my master's love.
> As I am a woman (now alas the day!),
> What thriftless sighs shall poor Olivia breathe!
> O Time, thou must untangle this, not I;
> It is too hard a knot for me t' untie!   (II.ii.34–42)

She sees the comedy and the pathos in the predicaments of others clearly because she is never selfishly strident about her own. Contrast Malvolio, blinded by self-love. Only egotistical myopia keeps Orsino from recognizing who it really is that

> never told her love,
> But let concealment, like a worm i' th' bud,
> Feed on her damask cheek. She pin'd in thought;

> And, with a green and yellow melancholy,
> She sat like Patience on a monument,
> Smiling at grief.   (II.iv.113–118)

Viola's way with grief is the way of humor and wisdom. When Olivia, hopelessly enamored of Cesario, cries that "a cypress, not a bosom, / Hides my heart," Viola has three words of absolute felicity, this time for another's predicament: "I pity you" (III.i.134). Rosalind as Ganymede, first wooed by Orlando pretending to address Rosalind and then pursued by infatuated Phebe, seems artificial beside Viola as Cesario with Olivia enamored. The seasoned wit of all three ladies makes that of *Love's Labour's Lost* seem like "taffeta phrases, silken terms precise, / Three-pil'd hyperboles, spruce affectation, / Figures pedantical." Viola's gentle humor and incisive wit lightly expose the absurdity of Orsino and Olivia on their vulnerable sentimental sides—the one in love with being in love, the other unseasonably in love with her memory of a dead brother, and both ending ironically with chance partners whom they never dreamed of drawing in the lottery of love. Viola's humor even discovers the vulnerable spot in Feste's omnipresent wit: "They that dally nicely with words may quickly make them wanton" (III.i.16–18). Her markmanship is not only excellent in shooting at the absurd; it is always humanized by the playfulness of humor, respectful of time and place. Hence she knows the secret of a fool's success in his fooling:

> He must observe their mood on whom he jests,
> The quality of persons, and the time;
> Not, like the haggard, check at every feather
> That comes before his eye.   (III.i.69–72)

Attitude and point of view in time, as I have insisted, are almost all, if not all, in determining whether we find a thing tragic or variously comic. In our time's transshifting, one season calls for this perspective, another for that, in the tragicomedy of our life.

If we see Viola more in the round by comparing her way with Orsino and Olivia to Rosalind's way with Orlando and Phebe, we see better the basic pattern of the play entire—radically comic—if we compare its end with the finish of *The Comedy of Errors*. Both denouements resolve complex tangles of disguise and mistaken identity. But the earlier play never for long rises above farce in any area. In the later there is no flaw in the possible assumptions that we are asked to make: Sebastian has no way of knowing that Viola is masquerading as Cesario, his image; there is complete "economy in the hypothesis," and to gloss over improbabilities en route there are such fine strokes as the speeches of Viola (III.iv.414–419) and the Duke and Antonio (V.i.223–231).[36] The harmony in *Twelfth Night* is more capacious than that in any preceding fusion of the comic and its kin with romantic love and adventure. Music, dance, and poetry are blended in to make a romantic comedy par excellence.

Summary observations on the nature of Shakespeare's mature romantic comedies are in order.

In all of these comedies, story bases are drawn from the great storehouse of inherited romantic narrative or tradition. They are rich in situations potentially either tragic or comic, and in characters, often rudimentary, all of whom invite tragic or comic treatment: the amorous tangles of noble ladies with devoted or faithless lovers, disguises, mistaken identities, feuds and reconciliations, distant locales, and so on. In all, characters more or less wooden are repeatedly transformed into human beings credible in the playhouse, by strokes of the comic in the very meanings of that term as I have understood it. With them particularly does the comic spirit sport, now laughing at the illusions of pastoralism, now at the pretended independence of the sexes, and always at the egos of romantic lovers. In all the plays new characters rich in broadly comic appeal—chiefly earthy Englishmen—are created and intimately made to affect the fates of the romantic folk who at first look toward unhappy ends but come eventually to happy ones: Bottom, Launce, Moth, Launcelot Gobbo, Dogberry, William and Audrey, Sir Toby and Sir Andrew. In all, new and subordinate story interests are created and usually so woven into the base ones that they influence their endings. The weaving is made to involve radically comic situations like the baiting of Benedick and Beatrice, the wooing of Rosalind as Ganymede by Orlando, and the gulling of Malvolio. In two of the plays clever professional jesters spotlight the pretenses, the ironies, and the ambiguities in the natures and doings of the chief characters. They are mature tools of comic artistry, exposing the blunt facts amusingly at odds with social pretenses. When conventional conduct leads their masters into tangles potentially tragic, Feste and Touchstone expose them in their comic absurdity. In one play a nitwitted constable and his aides accidentally uncover a serious plot against their superiors by trapping the villains and indirectly forcing two amorous self-deceivers into each other's arms. Two heroines, Rosalind and Viola, have such mellow and far-reaching humor that they complement Touchstone and Feste in their comic functioning, the while they are themselves comical.

In all the plays the style is marked by keen and subtle wit, sometimes excessive and dated for modern tastes, but usually part and parcel of the characters who voice it. Such wit points up the comic clash of animal facts with civilized conventions; yet it also makes us aware of some sort of cohesion in the midst of the comic diversity of experience that it more or less nets, for it flashes before the mind's eye unsuspected identities amid the apparent diversity of things that forever bombard us. In contrast with the wit of Restoration comedy, this wit though often sharp is seldom cutting because imbedded in humor expressed in beautiful poetry, keyed to sweet and harmonizing music, and yielding often to joyous dancing. Such witty dialogue is pervaded by a joyousness of spirit, by merriment in the moment in spite of any shadows that the main plots cast. A broad and genial tolerance suffers fools and foolishness with good-natured laughter while it simultaneously feels (and makes us feel) their pathos within the web of convention and pretense in which as civilized beings all of us are inevitably caught, though initially as self-justified in being whatever we intrinsically are as any king or queen—or Santayana's pumpkin lying on the ground. That pervasive awareness of our comic existence within the tragic realm of truth is distilled out in the exquisite songs that capture the specific moods and tones of the plays at the junctures when they are heard. Is not the greatest common denominator of these songs their gay-sad-gay contemplation of this duality of human life? Just to recall the opening verses of some of them is to suggest as much: "Sigh no more, Ladies, sigh no more!," "Under the greenwood tree," "Blow, blow, thou winter wind," "It was a lover and his lass," "O mistress mine, where are you roaming?," "Come away, come away, death," and "When that I was and a little tiny boy." We have but to think of the absence of such songs in Restoration drama to know the expanded horizons that music and song give to Shakespeare's "reading of earth" in his romantic comedies.

It is hardly accidental that the dance is allied with music in the romantic comedies, particularly in the most mature— *Much Ado*, *As You Like It*, and *Twelfth Night*. The first two end in dancing; the merry pranksters in the third dance and sing while exalting "cakes and ale." Like no other art, the dance plunges the whole man into the flux of existence, the groundwork of all that is comic. One remembers how the dancer emerges as Yeats's "favorite image for organic unity":

> For the good are always the merry,
> Save by an evil chance,
> And the merry love the fiddle,
> And the merry love to dance:[37]

What is more, all these romantic comedies are particularly rich in idealizing love and the ironies and ambiguities into which it easily slips; all multiply or intensify them by disguise or mistaken identity; and in most chance and accident figure strategically. Love, surely, is that area of human life where animal facts and social conventions are most often at odds; it has long been comedy's happy hunting ground. In his romantic comedies Shakespeare's genius for comedy cultivates this ground more finely than it has ever been tilled. One hears sometimes the voice of the sanely corrective critic, never the voice of the harsh satirist, and almost constantly that of the wise humorist.

All's Well That Ends Well, Measure for Measure, and *Troilus and Cressida* are commonly classified as comedies, and certainly the first two move from potentially tragic tangles into happy endings with some broadly comic incidents en route. Recently Josephine Waters Bennett has so revealingly studied the first two plays as genuine comedies that they need no longer be labeled "dark" ones or "problem plays" as often they have been.[38] But although she discloses unappreciated comic values in the structures and characterizations of both, she would, I think, hardly hold that the comic as I have understood it permeates and transforms all their materials as it does nearly everything in the sequence of romantic comedies ending with *Twelfth Night.* One recalling the "summary observations" about the full-blown romantic comedies in the preceding paragraphs will see that there is at least some qualitative difference between the comic in the plays reviewed and the comic in the two in question. In them humor (as I have construed the term), aided by song and dance, does not equally mingle with radically comic strains to effect the mood of acceptance of the human lot that is dominant in the major romantic comedies.

Troilus and Cressida is wholly devoid of such qualities. It has been a "problem" play from the beginning and

remains one, at least for classifiers. It is placed ambigu-
ously between the histories and the tragedies in the First
Folio; it is omitted from its table of contents; and though
the title page of Quarto B describes it as a "Famous His-
torie," the preface to that quarto more than once refers
to it as a "comedy." O. J. Campbell has read it as Shakespeare's venture into such "comicall satyre" as Jonson
and Marston were making popular about the time it appeared.[39] Satiric scorn and derision do indeed pervade
the play in spite of powerful lyrical passages like those
on time and degree that rise above the confusions of "wars
and lechery." Greeks and Trojans alike are rebuked as
they go counter to right reason and follow blind honor
and desire. The scurrilous tongue of Thersites, heard all
along, is that of a satiric railer: "Lechery, lechery! still
wars and lechery! Nothing else holds fashion. A burning
devil take them!" (V.ii.195–197). Also a satiric tool, Pandarus undercuts any high romantic stature for lust-driven
Troilus and wanton Cressida. Pandarus ends the play with
jesting jibes aimed (apparently) at a first audience of
sophisticated young lawyers of the Inns of Court. The
futility we feel "is the logical end of a youth's love for
a faithless woman. Futility is the logical result of a war
waged by a mob of selfish individuals incapable of submit-
ting themselves to the discipline of leadership. Futility
is the logical denouement of a play organized and
developed in the manner of a satirical comedy fashioned
after Ben Jonson's 'comicall satyres.' "[40] Nowhere in the
play do we hear comic laughter, free and full-chested
before the absurdity of human follies; nowhere is there
humorous maintainance of conventions; repeatedly romantic love and adventure are cut down to the level of
lust and folly by the satiric.

Nor is the comic spirit dominant in *Cymbeline, The Winter's Tale, The Tempest, Pericles,* and *The Two Noble Kinsmen*
(the last a collaboration and *Pericles* possibly one). That
of romance is. These late plays are perhaps best called

romances, though some have called them tragicomedies more or less illustrative of John Fletcher's familiar description of the kind: "A tragi-comedy is not so called in respect of mirth and killing, but in respect it wants deaths, which is enough to make it no tragedy, yet brings some near it, which is enough to make it no comedy."[41] The shades of bear-eaten Antigonus and his dead Prince Mamillius, of Cloten and his wicked mother, and of Arcite would protest such a surface classification of their respective plays. An able recent editor of *The Tempest* reads it as a romance and helpfully defines the term as

> a mode of exhibiting the action of magical and moral laws in a version of human life so selective as to obscure, for the special purpose of concentrating attention on these laws, the fact that in reality their force is intermittent and only fitfully glimpsed. Thus, although we may believe that in the end the forces of fertility, or of plenty, triumph, and that it is a law of human life that they should do so, we would not hold it as a rational conviction that this must be so in every single case, of every individual; yet comedy by a formal law, proved by a few exceptions, ends in a feast or a wedding. In the same way we accept even more arbitrary devices, such as that of the crucial 'recognition' of tragedy and comedy, as formal laws corresponding to, and in some valuable way illuminating, diurnal forces which are intermittent and rarely visible. In the realm of what we agree to call romance these conventions are both more frequent and more arbitrary.[42]

We can, however, count these several late plays as comedies if we focus on their happy endings that come when repentance, forgiveness, and reconciliation have resolved all turbulence that has disrupted initial equilibrium. E. M. W. Tillyard writes revealingly of tragedy and comedy as alike presenting a social order first harmonious, then discordant, and thereafter restored with a difference.[43] He sees tragedy as throwing the emphasis upon the disruption by evil rampant and comedy as not probing any evil but stressing triumph over it by reconciliation and renewal. And he finds in Shakespeare's last plays

strains of tragic conflict, past and current, variously submerged in triumphant movement toward forgiveness,
acceptance, and rejuvenation. *The Tempest* is obviously
the maturest example of comedy so conceived. One may
accept such an understanding of the pattern of a comedy
and yet find but a minor measure of the radically comic
or the critically comic or of the humorous in these plays.
They are perhaps even richer in romantic adventure than
are the earlier comedies, if not so rich in the amusing
mutations of romantic love. The resolutions of these plays
hinge upon the marvelous and the supernatural as the
ends of the earlier ones do not (with the exception of
A Midsummer Night's Dream). Unlike most of the earlier
comedies, no one of the last plays has a radically comic
or farcical situation fundamental in its structure. Some
radically comic characters and situations do appear—
Autolycus in *The Winter's Tale,* Boult and his associates
in *Pericles,* and Caliban and the drunken seamen in *The
Tempest.* But Bottom, Dogberry, Touchstone, Sir Toby,
and their associates are far more potent comic figures.
Truth is, the perspective in the late romances is one that
looks over—though it does not overlook—truly comic as
well as deeply tragic angles on life to its totality (mostly
memorably in *The Tempest),* particularly to its rejuvenation
in young lovers who reconcile and replace their discordant
elders. Many students see this outlook as the finest fruition
of the broadly comic vision. And some find it akin to
tragic insight when, "all passion spent," we "see into
the life of things" and resign ourselves to the truth of
them, however sad, as a new and purged social order
emerges. Unquestionably, reconciliation, affirmation, and
renewal are the dominant notes in the denouements of
these late plays even more than they are in the early romantic comedies, yet with significant differences: evil in the
last plays is more foursquarely met before being transcended, if met without the exposure of its devastating
power that the great tragedies show in their breasting

of the truth, however dark. Moreover, these plays (*The Tempest* particularly) offer perennial attraction to students who seek meaningful patterns of myth and allegorical overtones in plays.

Frank Kermode in editing *The Tempest* has observed that criticism of it "varies between the allegorical and the apocalyptic."[44] In glancing further at this play as the best of the late romances, the one in which comic and romantic domains merge and are somehow transcended, I would avoid such extremes of criticism.

The Tempest seems to rise above earth in its view of human life there. Yet it keeps a significant base on the sea voyages by brave mariners who were revealing a new world far to the west of Shakespeare's England. Many books about them surrounded Shakespeare when he wrote and touched even the popular sermons of the day. Some details of the storm that unforgettably begins the play and the description of Prospero's island appear to have been suggested by several narrative reports in 1610 of the Bermuda discoveries and adventures of Sir George Somers in the preceding year. And Kittredge astutely writes: "Unquestionably he had talked with sailors in his time and he owes quite as much to such conversations as to anything that he read in the four narratives."[45] In creating a sense of renewal in *The Tempest* inseparable from young love superseding old hate, Shakespeare may owe something to an awareness of the new and promising world over the seas that he shared with his fellows.

In the play all suggestions of actual voyaging and adventuring across the seas, of such new "romance," are assimilated by traditional romance materials much like those that we have already met: a duke dispossessed of his dukedom long ago by a false brother and banished to a strange island where he has acquired magical powers; storm and apparent shipwreck near it; and love at first sight between the duke's daughter and a young prince just brought ashore by those powers. In the opening scene a bluff boatswain with blunt wit and humor defies the engulfing waves and, by rebuking his panicky king and companions, at once rivets those romantic figures to rough actuality. The boatswain's facing of bald facts recalls the gravediggers in *Hamlet;* he too so jests in the face of death as to diminish intrusive great folk who fear it. At his side wise old Gonzalo, humorously meeting whatever fortune is casting up, confronts shipwreck: "Now would I give a thousand furlongs of sea for an acre of barren ground —long heath, brown furze, anything. The wills above be done! But I would fain die a dry death" (I.i.67–70).

The second scene recounts essential action long past, characterizes godlike Prospero and his innocent daughter, and evokes Ariel and Caliban. Those creatures of air and earth play imponderable parts in giving *The Tempest* elusive meanings that still lure students into mazes of allegory and symbolism. Essential to the impact of the play are the finely lyrical strains developed by Miranda and Ferdinand in speeches of enraptured adoration of each other, and by Ariel's exquisite songs—"Come unto these yellow sands" and "Full fadom five thy father lies." Perhaps the latter song subtly suggests the "sea-changes" in character that come within the play; both songs do help make the sea an encompassing presence in it. The treatment of romantic love between Ferdinand and Miranda contrasts with the handling of such love in the mature early comedies. Prospero maneuvers its inception and wisely nurtures it: "At the first sight / They have chang'd eyes" (I.ii.440–441); "Poor worm, thou art infected! / This visitation shows it" (III.i.31–32). Miranda, gentle of heart and unsullied by the world, has "no ambition / To see a goodlier man" (I.ii.482–483) than Ferdinand. The candor of "Do you love me?" (III.i.67) addressed to Ferdinand recalls Juliet's directness with Romeo, and gives Miranda a touch of Juliet's warmth. Ferdinand calls Miranda "goddess" (I.ii.421), finds her "peerless, . . . created / Of every creature's best" (III.i.47–48). At least once, Miranda catches a half humorous perspective on herself: "But I prattle / Something too wildly, and my father's precepts / I therein do forget" (III.i.57–59). But humor does not play between her and Ferdinand to modify the romantic pitch of their love as it plays within Portia, Beatrice, Rosalind, and Viola, if not equally within the men they love. However, in Prospero's wise and omniscient detachment and sympathy there is much mature wit and humor as he beholds the intense young lovers with tender amusement. Miranda's instantly finding Ferdinand a paragon among men though he is but the third male creature she has seen since she was an infant has its comic aspect, somewhat ironically paralleled by Caliban's drunken adoration of drunken Stephano, the third man he has known: a "most ridiculous monster, to make a wonder of a poor drunkard" (II.ii.169–170), as tipsy Trinculo declares. The three roisterers plot to slay Prospero even as wicked Sebastian and Antonio plot to kill Alonso and Gonzalo, but our knowledge that Prospero's "so potent art" controls all action on the island keeps all evil there within comic confines. The farcical antics of the drunken trio give us free moments of radical comedy. Trinculo cries: "They say there's but five upon this isle. We are three of them. If th' other two be brain'd like us, the state totters" (III.ii.6–8). His "Any strange beast there makes a man" (II.ii.33) recalls the gravedigger in *Hamlet* gibing at England as the land of madmen. Disguise, ancient vehicle of the radically comic, appears when Caliban and Trinculo, joined to seem a four-footed and two-voiced beast when the former hides under the latter's gaberdine, are mistaken for just such by Stephano. In them, drink once more floats the radically comic. Their comic confusion takes a further turn as Stephano and Caliban think Trinculo interrupts their chatter when actually invisible Ariel is gulling the three of them.

But it is not in its farcical characters that the play has its great power. It is in dominant Prospero and the romantic figures around him as they complement and illuminate his attitude toward life that, looking beyond the merely comic, the purely tragic, and the naively romantic, fructifies in the wisdom of forgiveness and resignation. Mellow humor and unselfish love give Viola understanding and wisdom, but in a world without rampant evil. Prospero attains such virtues in a world with evil active in it, and after a far wider sweep of experience. He will justly have his dukedom back:

> I do forgive
> Thy rankest fault—all of them; and require
> My dukedom of thee, which perforce I know
> Thou must restore.   (V.i.131–134)

But Ariel as Prospero's servant and a "minister of Fate" tells Alonso, Sebastian, and Antonio that they need "nothing but heart's sorrow / And a clear life ensuing" (III.iii.81–82) to be saved from due punishment for their having supplanted "good Prospero." When Ariel declares that, were he human, his affections would extend to the distressed king and his evil associates, Prospero exclaims:

> And mine shall.
> Hast thou, which art but air, a touch, a feeling
> Of their afflictions, and shall not myself,
> One of their kind, that relish all as sharply
> Passion as they, be kindlier mov'd than thou art?
> Though with their high wrongs I am struck to th' quick,
> Yet with my nobler reason 'gainst my fury
> Do I take part. The rarer action is
> In virtue than in vengeance. They being penitent,
> The sole drift of my purpose doth extend
> Not a frown further.   (V.i.20–30)

Prospero's forgiveness is based on knowledge, self-discipline, and charity, not on ignorance or innocence; so too his sympathy and understanding:

> *Mir.*   O, wonder!
> How many goodly creatures are there here!

> How beauteous mankind is! O brave new world
> That has such people in't!
> *Pros.*   'Tis new to thee.   (V.i.181–184)

Viola's understanding and sympathy yield her "I pity you"
for infatuated Olivia; Prospero's "'Tis new to thee" adds
high wisdom touched with humor and irony. Moreover,
wit can season his gravity: having just "lost" his beloved
daughter to Ferdinand, he plays lightly with Alonso's
"loss" of his "dear son Ferdinand"; he will now "bring
forth a wonder to content ye / As much as me my dukedom" (V.i.170–171). Ultimate comic vision looks not to
yesterday but to today: Prospero meets Alonso's lament
that he must ask his child's forgiveness: "There, sir, stop.
/ Let us not burthen our remembrance with / A heaviness
that's gone" (V.i.198–200).

The wisdom and humor, the forgiveness and understanding in Prospero gain added body by being exemplified also in old Gonzalo. In the witty dialogue wherein
he portrays an ideal commonwealth his "good nature and
kindly feeling . . . are finely contrasted with the sneering
cynicism of the treacherous Antonio and the unprincipled
Sebastian."[46] That portrait subtly enhances the suggestion
of the new and better order the young lovers inaugurate
to supplant the old in which evil triumphed. Gonzalo's
blessing of them, which surveys the way fate has ironically
but happily resolved all, may suggest to a reader Hamlet's
"There's a divinity that shapes our ends, / Rough-hew
them how we will" (V.ii.10–11):

> Look down, you gods,
> And on this couple drop a blessed crown!
> For it is you that have chalk'd forth the way
> Which brought us hither.   (V.i.201–204)

This sense of harmony emergent from a world wherein
evil has run rampant comes in *The Tempest* partly because
of the pervasiveness of music in it—music, Shakespeare's
"recurrent symbol of harmony," as has been noted.[47]

"Music is of great importance in *The Tempest*, which contains more songs than any other play, and which often demands instrumental music also."[48] Moreover, these songs have been "justly appraised . . . as of a kind written by Shakespeare only at the end of his career—'set songs so deeply embedded in the text as dialogue that it is unnecessary to stop the action to permit them to be performed, for they are essentially a part of it.' "[49] Music "solemn," "strange," "soft," "heavenly," or "marvelously sweet" is repeatedly heard. Farcical Caliban and Stephano sing when drunk. Surely it is not without significance that the reconciling power of music stirs even earthbound Caliban. His beautiful verses telling of "sounds and sweet airs that give delight and hurt not" and "a thousand twangling instruments" that "will hum about mine ears" (III.ii.145–147) show that he, "despite his inherited malignity, has a childlike susceptibility to music; and this suggests that he is a child in other respects, and therefore not incapable of moral development."[50]

Contributing also to the embracive feeling of reconcilement in the play is the presence of sleep, of dreams and dreaming—favorite themes in Elizabethan poetry. Sweet music that comes to Caliban when he is dreaming leads him when he wakes to cry to dream again.[51] Ariel charms to sleep the mariners when he brings the king's ship to harbor. The mystery of sleep, of dreaming, and of waking is relevant to Alonso and Gonzalo and, from another angle, to the conspirators Antonio and Sebastian when they seek the lives of those slumberers in II.i. Miranda remembers "the dark backward and abysm of time" before she and her father came to the island: "Tis far off, / And rather like a dream than an assurance / That my remembrance warrants" (I.ii.44–46). Ferdinand cries "My spirits, as in a dream, are all bound up" (I.ii.486) when Prospero has him *charmed from moving.* Sleep and dreams and music permeating the play give it some of the sense of harmony in spite of any discords that uniquely marks it and helps lift it above all the comic and tragic experiences of life. Prospero's celebrated verses beginning "Our revels now are ended" come inevitably to mind. They focus the over-arching view of life that the play often brings: "We are such stuff / As dreams are made on, and our little life / Is rounded with a sleep" (IV.i.156–158).

Dancing, close ally of the comic spirit as Yeats has reminded us, is restricted to extraneous characters in *The Tempest:* the Strange Shapes (III.iii) and the Reapers and Nymphs (IV.i). Central characters, significantly, do not dance merrily at the end of the play as they do in several of the early comedies.

Marvelous adventure and idealizing love are finely il-lustrated in *The Tempest*. And magic—beneficent white magic—rules both as in no other play. This hoary tool of high romance is instrumental in Prospero's effecting his commendable ends wherein justice is tempered with mercy and magnanimity, and rule passes to the unspoiled young. We are free to deny the validity today of such a triumph over adversity through an instrument long dis-credited for us.[52] And we are free to allegorize and moralize after almost any fashion (as too many have) the meaning of the magic in Prospero's scheme of things, to rationalize it into our own if we will. Yet we are equally free to rest with the play as it overtly tells any man of possible triumph by his "nobler reason" when he seeks to do justice and love mercy, know humor, and through study and discipline attain the calm of the philosophic mind. Thus he may find what will suffice. And his children who suc-ceed him as he retires (like Prospero) from the stage of life give him a certain vicarious immortality.

Like the mature romantic comedies, this best of the romances encompasses the wisdom of humor and does not disdain the fun of lowly farce. However, by a radical infusion of the wonder and power of the maternal sea, of exalted romantic love, of magic, of sleep, of dreams, and of music it acquires antennae that reach over the confines of both the comic and the tragic to the ultimate mystery and eventual peace beyond "this insubstantial pageant faded."

In the early romantic comedies, humor, usually running hand in hand with the radically comic, lively wit, a mild measure of the correctively comic, and very little of the satiric, effects the reconciliation. Humor is not absent from the romances; but in them reconciliation and a sense of continuing life come through crucial interventions of the marvelous or supernatural: "Apparitions" in *Cymbeline*, Diana in *Pericles*, Apollo's Oracle in *The Winter's Tale*, Hymen and the gods in *The Two Noble Kinsmen*, and (most memorably) Prospero with his white magic in *The Tempest*. Perhaps the pervasive humor of the earlier romantic comedies is more relevant to our lot today when the natural constantly encroaches upon the traditionally supernatural—and reason and humor will save us if saved we are to be.

CHAPTER V

The COMIC UNCONFINED: FALSTAFF

Sir Toby Belch has an elder brother in Sir John Falstaff. He lives in a milieu completely shorn of the romantic, adventurous or amorous. His "amours" with Dame Quickly and Doll Tearsheet are as far from those of traditional romance as a knight's can get; so, too, his doings on Gadshill, in the Boar's Head Tavern, and at Shrewsbury. Falstaff illustrates the comic divorced from any corrective or satiric intent; but he remains monarch absolute over all the realms of the radically comic, the humorous, and the witty. Irony does eventually enfold him, though (ironically) not a comic irony. And, supreme comic character, he inevitably arises and flourishes in the world of actuality that the history plays, tethered to it, refract.

Rotund Falstaff may be approached from many angles; witness the various critics from Maurice Morgann in 1777 on down.[1] By facing the old question "Is Falstaff a coward?"[2] I shall try to take his comic girth before turning to comic strains in the tragedies.

We recall Santayana's assertions that "pure comedy is scornful, merciless, devastating, holding no door open to anything beyond. . . . [It is] the irresponsible, complete, extreme expression of each moment."[3] Though a ton of

125

a man from one angle (as a sustained character in a playhouse drama), from another, Falstaff is primarily a tool of the purely comic, his habitat the comic moment. As such a dramatic device he is the ultimate descendant of the *miles gloriosus*, the Vice of the old moralities, and most fools and jesters, as many students have repeatedly pointed out. If we realize that his basic footing is in this realm, in which all human doings, considered outwardly, are absurd and laughable, his disrespect for valor and honor—for anything so long as in the extant moment he may amuse and be amused by the absurd spectacle—will agitate us less. As an instrument of the radically comic, something less than a man if we insist on looking at him always through moralizing eyes forever in focus for the world's work, Falstaff is ready to sport with anything, to unmask rudely the animal fact behind the man-made convention or fiction, to laugh robustly at it in the moment, and then (complicating matters because involving time and hence character) to suffer it playfully over time as a humorist. Recall his devastating disquisition on honor; recall his brutal way with those "pitiful rascals" of "the King's press" as "food for powder, food for powder" that will "fill a pit as well as better"; recall his merciless scalping of Justice Shallow—that yet yields to humorous sufferance of his fatuousness.

When Falstaff flees at Gadshill we should remember that the mere animal man, living instinctively in the instant, never stands and fights against odds if he feels that he can save his skin by running—is a "coward on instinct." Honor, like pity, is a learned virtue. At Gadshill and at Shrewsbury Shakespeare is giving us great jokes if we but have eyes to see them; and they are grounded, as all jokes are, in the flying moment in which instinctive life pulses heedless of all form, propriety, and convention, and in ridiculous contrast with them.

Of Gadshill Kittredge wrote that the "point of the jest lies, not in Falstaff's taking to his heels, but in his upbraid-

ing the Prince and Poins for cowardice and thus enabling
them to turn the tables; for it was he who ran—not they."[4]
Just so? The point of all this jesting is surely lost in the
theater unless Falstaff's running is accepted as cowardly,
as it always has been by actor folk and audiences.[5] That
running is the hub of Falstaff as a radically comic device,
his primary nature; it is only by way of the "convention"
of courage "thrown over altogether" by animal instinct
in the moment that a comic contrast can here be operative.
Kittredge's defense of Falstaff,[6] now at Gadshill as "not
a soldier on guard, bound, if need be, to sacrifice his
life for his country," but "a highwayman in danger of
arrest—and the penalty for robbery was hanging," then
at Shrewsbury as a "veteran officer who has had fighting
enough in the past and does not love danger for its own
sake"—as "not a coward in fact"—slips out of the realm of
comic contrast and dramatic illusion into character in
workaday life. As Stoll has insisted, "fact" is not in question; "the essence of comedy"—"the sharp, abrupt contrast between appearance and fact and the swift transition
from one to the other"[7]—is; an artistic, dramatic device
is, an age-old comic one, both larger and less than life—the
stock coward. Falstaff fleeing is precisely that. The trouble
arises for Kittredge and our modern sensibilities in the
sustained portrayal of Falstaff that makes him something
beyond just that, as I shall shortly insist.[8]

When we follow Falstaff through his irresponsible sporting in the midst of battle and everywhere else, we should
never once forget this aspect of him as a tool of the purely
comic (a clown par excellence), operative in the extant
moment in which animal life ignores all moral accretions
vital to social life over time, in which for the nonce workaday values are rudely unsaddled. In it, the animal man
concerns himself with the free play of life in radical contrast
with any and all social constructs suddenly thrown by
it into absurd relief. In that amoral moment all jests and
jokes arise; it is the native habitat of clowns; neither cow-

ardice nor courage is relevant. Sheer amusement is all—or should be. One "does not quarrel with a clown for lack of moral sense, unless the dramatist fails to make this want amusing."[9] And who will say that Shakespeare for a second fails to make Falstaff's want of such a sense amusing? Although Lamb violently uprooted Restoration comedy from its soil, he had too keen an intuition of the essence of the comic not to understand that the elemental sort sidesteps in the moment our workaday moral world —perhaps, one might moralize, to humble our perspective on it. The comic has its *point d'appui* in the rushing, irrational instant of existence that is antecedent to morality, though that instant is the base of morality as the moment spreads out into the entanglements of time.

But of course no full-bodied figure in life or in drama can abide only in the isolated moment; for character is in essence the moral accretion of all a man's moments as over time they mesh together to tell his full tale in the realm of truth. Falstaff, nascently a comic device whose milieu is the amoral comic moment, is also a rotund dramatic character so sustained over a few hours of stage traffic as to suggest long life through time. As such, he is, paradoxically if you please, an individual of enormous girth, captivating all of us by his endless zest for life, his dauntless wit, and his irrepressible humor—and caught in time like the rest of us. Who does not prefer the company of this "gross fat man" to that of his betters? It is, I think, this "plump Jack"—feasting, drinking, wenching, swaggering, and joking with matchless wit through time—that has dazzled the vision of some critics into forgetting his primary function as the radically comic device that I have focused on.[10] Truth is, Shakespeare so richly develops this man Falstaff, this "huge hill of flesh," beyond that device that his defenders against all comers forget his basic footing as the latter, and hence throw out of focus his comic cowardice.[11] Bounding good nature, humorously maintaining the conventions and hence radiating out into time, and expressed by an inexhaustible wit, wins our admiration and affection in spite of the rascality and cowardice. The appealing wit and humor somehow run *pari passu* in the playhouse with the merely comic—the genial sufferance with the blunt exposure; so we accept the old sinner as we grow fond of the man.

And yet the roundness and rightness of Shakespeare's portrayal of Falstaff appear if we pursue the man to his end. This "whoreson round man" flourishing over time is incorrigibly bent on not looking before and after the moment and his favorite drink in it, sack strongly laced with the radically comic. It is not by accident that this king of the comic has a tankard often at his lips. Drink, we all know, is an eye-opener for facts behind appearances—or an irresponsible juggler with those facts to breed more illusions than the conventions it unseats. Falstaff's constant imbibing of his heady brew leads him to more than myopia as time with its inevitable net of conventions that he flaunts closes around him in Henry V's cry "I know thee not, old man!" By this point Falstaff the man —the sustained character that Shakespeare has over time humanized with irresistible wit and humor—is drunk of an excessive intake of the comic, "infatuated," as Kittredge aptly put it.[12] A clown, old and gray, has become the "dupe of his egotism" and forgotten that his ridiculous fellows are "living quite in earnest" with their "absurd" conventions of honor and respectability.[13] He who has seen the absurd side of everything, including courage and honor, has gone blind to his own. Held in defiance of life's shifting and multiple needs, the comic stance becomes itself a "convention," itself absurd beside those changing, manifold needs. The persistently comic posture is no wiser in our moving existence if its moral fabric is to cohere than any other gone rigid; to everything its season. Too late he who has grown fat and grey on the comic discovers that, old and alone, he cannot live otherwise in a moral world in which time turns playboy princes into dutiful kings who must get on with the world's work. An essential irony of existence overtakes Falstaff the man. His convention-minded cronies have twitted him as a coward; but duty and honor have never bothered him. His cry has always been: "Give me life; which if I can save, so; if not, honour comes unlook'd for, and there's an end." Now Hal, become king, casts off the absurd old sot who has blindly forgotten that his irresponsible way of life in which a madcap prince may indulge for a season cannot encroach on a monarch's. How could it be otherwise if life as all of us must live it is not to be falsified? If we feel the pathos of Falstaff's plight, we should see the inevitability of it—its fidelity to things as they are.[14]

Such consummate humanization of this comic device, this cowardly clown of complex ancestry, reaches another marvelously pathetic pitch when Dame Quickly reports the death of Falstaff to his preposterous cronies. There comes "an extraordinary scene—beyond question one of the most wonderful in Shakespeare. In mourning for Falstaff all these comic characters speak in accordance with their several whimsicalities of style and manner—Pistol rants, alliterates, and defies logic ('Bardolph be blithe; . . . for Falstaff he is dead, And we must ern therefore'), the Hostess mixes up her words and speaks with ludicrous ambiguity, the Page pokes fun at Bardolph's nose and Bardolph resents it with his usual irascibility. Nothing could be more wildly comic than what is said; yet the general effect is that of almost unendurable pathos."[15] No wonder learned men cogitating in their studies lose perspective on Falstaff clowning in the theater; such scenes pondered so win us to love of the grand old sinner that with "plump Jack" banished from life, all the world of jollity and free-living fun seems gone too. Bardolph's cry is ours: "Would I were with him wheresom'er he is, whether in heaven or in hell!" We forget the sins of "that reverend vice, that grey iniquity, that father ruffian, that

vanity in years" in these superbly comic moments that
great art simultaneously shows in their pathetic aspect
as well. Do not the pathetic and the comic touch in that
both in their purity breed fundamental humility before
the inexplicable rush of events in this our life, the former
with an awareness of our ultimate helplessness to swim
against them, and the latter with an awareness of our
paradoxical freedom to laugh out before the absurdity of
all human constructs upon them—foam churned up by
the tumbling waves? Should not the upshot for the spirit
in both instances be humility in breasting those tides
that engender it, buoy it up, and sweep it away? Be these
large questions as they may, Shakespeare, unlike the comic
colossus that he has created, is Santayana's "just critic
of life" and "good philosopher," for he has seen "the
absurdity, and understood the life."[16] So should we see
the clown, and understand the man. Then the moral issues—the cowardice in particular—will cease to trouble
us.

We who are forever freer from care because Falstaff
forever spurned it as an enemy to life, lived not wisely
as this world goes but too well as a clown of consummate
wit and jollity, can well leave this mere shadow of imagination to rest in the green fields of which Theobald in his
celebrated emendation set him babbling at his end. If
Leslie Hotson would deny him just those fields,[17] no one
would refuse him the perennially green ones of art. To
our abiding delectation, there at least neither cowardice
nor honor in reality comes near the radically comic
moments that are the primary habitat of this supreme
stage clown, however closely we mere mortals must hug
our conventions of honor and respectability to survive
in our off-stage world. Falstaff, unlike the lot of us, is
no mere mortal to be weighed always in the scales of
our concepts of right and wrong, though by his maker
he is quite rightly judged at the finish because great art
is ultimately tethered to truth stretched tragically over

time. He is primarily a comic device or tool; his milieu is stage plays that refract rather than reflect our life, slipping free, to our abiding delight and refreshment, of the noose of all our conventions for irresponsible, momentary existence—then supremely humanized as a dramatic character caught in their coils at last.[18]

I have dissected not to murder, but to understand. The comic skeleton of Falstaff is embedded in humorous flesh and blood, a "huge hill" of it.[19]

The upshot of Shakespeare's artistry is a king, every pound of him, of the comic, the humorous, and the witty alike—with a poignant dash of pathos about his end. Yet he remains but a playhouse shadow of the absurd shadows that we ourselves cast. Hence we are free, perhaps, to let our fancy range for a final moment over a shadow that is of imagination all compact. Whether or not he is a coward troubles Falstaff not at all. He is still ready heedlessly to appear one to add to the fun of things. Need we nowadays be more troubled about the business than he is? Could we now have our playhouse fun with him did he not still run away on Gadshill and revive at Shrewsbury so careless of honor yet so captivating in wit and humor that learned folk have now held him a coward, and now not—and will no doubt comically continue to worry the point? His stentorian laughter one can almost hear.[20]

CHAPTER VI

The COMIC and
the TRAGIC: *Hamlet*

In turning from Falstaff to comic strains in Shakespearean tragedy, we might well recall what was said at the outset about the nearness of the comic to the tragic.[1] As Santayana declares, the comic is the "irresponsible, complete, extreme expression of each moment" in which we are aware of the absurd contrast between the existential fact and the encrusting convention; the humorous emerges when we look at that contrast with understanding enough to maintain the convention in spite of the absurdity. The correctively comic uses that mere awareness of the absurdity of the conventional to laugh us out of excessive gaps between sane facts and foolish forms. It shades into the satiric when intent would rebuke vice and folly with more or less ire and indignation. The tragic probes the destructiveness of those vices and follies that the hotly satiric chastises. It asks why and wherefore "in this our life" where "passions spin the plot." It appears when creatures who must persist beyond any free comic moments find themselves fatally enmeshed over long time in the jungle of existence wherein they perforce reckon with the moral involvements of their actions. The heroically tragic (Shakespeare's, for example), known to our turbulent century of the common man more by inheritance than by creation of it, traditionally centers on an essentially noble protagonist caught in a jam of good and evil and struggling disastrously through to self-knowledge and the truth.

Forced to act without seeing clearly just where his freedom ends and his fate cries out, he must make us feel in the tension of his predicament a magnified version of our own. The spectacle of his suffering must arouse in us pity and fear—Horatio's "woe and wonder" are words that some find apt for Shakespearean tragedy.[2] The vision of the full truth to which the protagonist finally attains must expand our awareness of the paradoxical nature of man:

> Chaos of thought and passions, all confused;
> Still by himself abused or disabused;
> Created half to rise, and half to fall;
> Great lord of all things, yet a prey to all;
> Sole judge of truth, in endless error hurl'd;
> The glory, jest, and riddle of the world![3]

And we must become aware of the valiancy of our dust even in its defeat.[4]

If *King Lear* in its depth and epic sweep heightens our tragic awareness more than any of Shakespeare's tragedies, *Hamlet* has long come closer to the bosoms of men than any tragedy in the world. Modern man finds it almost a paradigm of his tragic experience of life.[5] And Polonius and the gravediggers give the common reader more obvious comic amusement than he finds in any other of Shakespeare's major tragedies. Hence I shall look with some care at the comic in *Hamlet*, but only glance at *Romeo and Juliet* (its Nurse and Mercutio), *Othello* (its clown and Vice-descended villain), *Macbeth* (its drunken porter), *Antony and Cleopatra* (its clown, its messenger, its choruslike Enobarbus, and its queen with a comic dimension whatever her grandeur), and *Lear* (its supreme fool). The most discussed of plays will remain the most fascinating, however inept my touch with it may be.

The wonderful opening scene of *Hamlet*, dark and foreboding, embraces but one speech with a comic cast: Horatio's "A piece of him" in response to Bernardo's "What, is Horatio there?" This "mildly jocose" or humorous remark helps to round out a character who all along will embody sense, whatever the tangle of sense and sensibility around him.[6] Everything else in this scene is grave and ominous. Soon the first formal court since Claudius ascended the throne shows him a master of affairs, yet inadvertently brushing with Hamlet. But this scene has no moment of true humor. Hamlet's puns on "kin," "kind," and "sun" are bitterly in key with his grief for his dead father and disgust with his mother's "o'erhasty marriage." Shortly his first great soliloquy plunges us into a private tragic realm wherein his long view of "all the uses of this world" finds them "weary, stale, flat, and unprofitable." He greets Horatio, Marcellus, and Bernardo with his accustomed graciousness; but vibrating sorrow and disillusionment quickly surface again in his interchange with his old friend:

> *Hor.* My lord, I came to see your father's funeral.
> *Ham.* I prithee do not mock me, fellow student.
> I think it was to see my mother's wedding.   (I.ii.176–178)

The rest of the scene is tense with the report of the ghost and with Hamlet's eagerness to confront it.

Freely comic material first emerges at the outset of scene iii in the amusing deflation of Laertes by Ophelia when her counsel that he "reck" his own "rede" after he has lectured her at length on right conduct makes him suddenly discover that he has stayed "too long." Shortly Polonius is giving his famous advice to his advising son and counseling his daughter as a circumspect father might.

All of us laugh at Polonius as a figure of high comedy, yet harmoniously a part of a high tragedy. Dr. Johnson put the comic point of him in four words—"dotage encroaching upon wisdom."[7] That dotage repeatedly amuses us in his fondness for lecturing and giving advice, however sound, to his meandering young; in his losing the line of his thought in converse with Reynaldo and over-elaborating it in speech with his king and queen; in his swallowing all of Hamlet's "mad" talk (if, perhaps, with an intent to humor his seemingly insane prince); and in his tenacious pursuit of his *idée fixe* that spurned love lies behind Hamlet's apparent madness. In all such behavior he stimulates acutely our sense of the absurd gap between shifting animal facts and desiccated forms.

But in amusement before the comic stature of Polonius we should not miss his dimension as a figure in a playhouse tragedy that involves various individuals and groups of individuals disastrously. He is no mere comic appendage to it; he is an organic part of it as well as its most deliciously comic character. His accidental death by Hamlet's sword plunging for Claudius may be seen as the crisis of the play. We obscure the rounded role of Polonius in a uniquely complicated drama if we dismiss him as no more than a "foolish prating knave," a "wretched, rash, intruding fool," mistaken for his better.[8]

Polonius has a minor tragic dimension as well as a major comic; our eyes catch a complete view of him that Hamlet's cannot in such phrases. Apart from the flatness of Polonius seen as no more than a doddering old fool, we lose the rich orchestration of the tragedy if we miss some of his notes in it by ignoring the varied comments on him that flesh him out into a complex creature, caught fumbling in a world he never made and unwittingly helping to weave the fine mesh of ironic contrasts essential in great tragic drama. For an unprejudiced audience Polonius has some dignity as well as much dotage. The throne defers to his wishes for his son; Claudius tells Laertes:

> The head is not more native to the heart,
> The hand more instrumental to the mouth,
> Than is the throne of Denmark to thy father.   (I.ii.47–49)

Polonius's prohibitions to Ophelia are indeed disastrous, timed ironically as they are; yet they are made by a loving father solicitous for the welfare of his daughter. He does stoop to conquer in sending a servant to "spy" on Laertes; but he is, even so, a circumspect parent concerned about the right development of a son who later proves putty in villainous hands. Polonius's wrong conclusion about Hamlet's madness is more in key with a dramatist's intent to multiply tragic-comic irony than the mark of a fool. His garrulity and vanity are indeed very comically illustrative of his dotage—actuality slipping through his fingers as he gives us "words, words, words." Spying twice behind an arras, though it certainly does not dignify Polonius, is yet the move of a counselor sincerely concerned according to his lights to help his king (of whose villainous conduct he of course has no faintest suspicion, as commentators often forget) cure seemingly dangerous madness in his prince.[9] His place at court as the righthand counselor of its sovereign appears to an unbiased audience that of a respected elder statesman—no more inept than some such dignitaries at any time. Claudius and Gertrude always pay Polonius due respect, if tolerantly aware of the "dotage encroaching upon wisdom." Hamlet's rude cry "These tedious old fools!" (II.ii.223) as Polonius is leaving him just after Rosencrantz and Guildenstern enter is part of his "mad" talk. Gertrude remembers a "good old man." And his death without dignity is a part of the web of tragic irony, not deliberate degradation of him because he is no more than a "wretched, rash, intruding fool." Those words express Hamlet when he is furious with frustration because his sword has missed Claudius, not his reasoned judgment on the complete man. And, if it does not follow that because his children loved him Polonius must therefore have been worthy of their devotion, it hardly follows that he was unworthy of it although they did love him. The father's death precipitates madness in one child and headlong vengeance in the other.

A rounded view of Polonius recognizes in him a preeminently comic figure depicted with enough dignity to fix him firmly in the tragic involvement that brings his ironic death and to draw at least a bit of our feeling of the pity of it all. Portrayals have too often made a mere caricature of him. Critical dismissal of him as a fool and knave pushes him toward the realm of the satiric butt, scorned and derided; Hamlet's hot words over his body are hardly the sum of the matter for the spectator of the tragedy entire. If no dignity or wisdom in Polonius is made manifest in the play for dotage to encroach upon, what becomes of his comic aspect that must turn upon a blunt (and evident) contrast between changing animal fact and accrued social form and convention? Dr. Johnson's words are just. They keep Polonius in the realm of high comedy and within the involution of tragic ironies that make up the fabric of *Hamlet*.

Seeing Polonius as a comic figure with a firm footing in a tragic world reminds us anew how near allied are the tragic and the comic aspects of any given object in nature. A nice instance of the sustaining of a comic view of Polonius against a background of tragic involvement is the baiting dialogue with its *double-entendres* in III.ii. It has none of the free and irresponsible play of the radically comic; Hamlet's gulling of Polonius cuts with a satiric edge within its "mad" style. Even as his "mad" talk in casting off Ophelia vibrates with satiric-tragic awareness —her predicament is one into which a generous lover cannot reasonably be expected to draw her—so does his bawdy jesting with her on the eve of the dumb show—and so does his jesting with Rosencrantz and Guildenstern in II.ii. The underside of such wit is not comic awareness; grave tensions spreading over time undercut any comic impact in it; there is no free play about it. The satiric strain in Hamlet has been ably isolated by O. J. Campbell. Repeatedly Hamlet "parries the heaviest blows of adversity by wielding the familiar weapons of the mocking satirist." Under cover of his "antic disposition" he shoots his barbed satiric darts at Polonius, at Gertrude and Claudius, at Rosencrantz and Guildenstern, at Osric, and at Ophelia. Bitter disillusionment and disgust with his murderous uncle and incestuous mother animate such cutting thrusts; they make him a cousin to Malevole in John Marston's *The Malcontent* in his invectives against the corruption of mankind. "Hamlet's irresistible impulse toward mockery delays the catastrophe and so prolongs and complicates the suspense." Moreover, "Hamlet's bursts of righteous indignation help Shakespeare to create the illusion that Hamlet is endowed with an infinitely rich and sensitive nature. What in Malevole is the railing of a disappointed, ill-natured cynic becomes in Hamlet the deepest and most moving philosophical lyricism in all literature."[10]

Perhaps nowhere in Shakespeare do the tragic and the radically comic outlooks confront each other so directly as in V.i. of *Hamlet*.[11] In joking about drowning, burial, hanging, and their immemorial profession of grave-digging, the two clowns have the unmitigatedly comic angle on all mortality. They look directly at the blunt facts of mortal life, utterly absurd, yet take them in stride with liberating drink and song.

> *Ham.* Has this fellow no feeling of his business, that he sings at grave-making?
> *Hor.* Custom hath made it in him a property of easiness.
> *Ham.* 'Tis e'en so. The hand of little employment hath the daintier sense.   (V.i.74–78)

The "daintier sense" that gives the full tragic awareness of life—classically expressed in Hamlet's great soliloquies—is not for the horny-handed gravediggers; to them another skull is just another spadeload of dirt in their day's work. But the skull once beneath the fair skin triggers Hamlet into musing on Cain's jawbone, a politician's pate, and Lord Such-a-one—all now "my Lady Worm's, chapless, an knock'd about the mazzard with a sexton's spade." Here is indeed a "fine revolution, an we had the trick to see't"! The humble gravediggers have the "trick" or knack of the freely comic denied the "daintier sense" of the prince who takes the long and tragic perspective of the truth; he neglects the radically comic dimension of the skull in looking all around for its truth rather than freely and directly at it in the extant moment. His live bones ache to think that these grave-bones "cost no more the breeding but to play at loggets with 'em." When the singing clown tosses up another skull, Hamlet meditates anew on the sad and ironic mutations of man's dust: "This fellow might be in's time a great buyer of land, with his statutes, his recognizances, his fines, his double vouchers, his recoveries. Is this the fine of his fines, and the recovery of his recoveries, to have his fine pate full of fine dirt?" But Hamlet's "fine" ironic meditation and word play are broken off abruptly by the flowing present in which a clown ironically and comically outdoes a prince in wit by turning his quick earthy sense on him, quite mad so the clown (ironically) thinks and (ironically again) quite unrecognized because he was thought to have been sent into England to recover his wits, where if he "do not, 'tis no great matter there," for "there the men are as mad as he." This thrust at the English is a genuinely comic moment that rises tangentially free of the tragic-comic-ironic setting of the repartee between prince and clown. But the irony strikes again when the clown turns up Yorick's skull and Hamlet ponders the reduction of this "fellow of infinite jest, of most excellent fancy" to a spadeful of dirt:

> He hath borne me on his back a thousand times. And now how abhorred in my imagination it is! My gorge rises at it. Here hung those lips that I have kiss'd I know not how oft. Where be your gibes now? your gambols? your songs? your flashes of merriment that were wont to set the table on a roar? Not one now, to mock your own grinning? Quite chapfall'n? Now get you to my lady's chamber, and tell her, let her paint an inch thick, to this favour she must come. Make her laugh at that.   (V.i.204–216)

The tragic and ironic angle on the human lot would seem to be the ultimate. But not quite so. Seeing Alexander's noble dust stopping a bunghole and seeing no more draws from Horatio the rational reply: " 'Twere to consider too curiously, to consider so." As Santayana (echoing Plato) declares, "unmitigated seriousness is always out of place in human affairs."[12] Yet your tragic hero will persist in his long dark view of the truth—until confronted by the blunt new fact of Ophelia's coffin and driven into melodramatic grappling with Laertes in her grave.

Beyond this encounter with the gravediggers there is no time for anything akin to the comic except the dialogue wherein Hamlet, now poised for his fate in knowing that "the readiness is all," is free enough to mock Osric's affectations in language and expose in them the comic gap between pretense and good sense. He baits this "waterfly" courtier somewhat as he earlier leads Polonius to see a cloud now as a camel, now as a weasel, and now as a whale; but there is less satiric bite in the baiting because of that new poise in Hamlet.[13]

Polonius, the gravediggers, and Osric in their comic dimensions not only make us smile in the midst of tragedy; they deepen our sense of the girth of Hamlet's awareness and of the sweep of his world, for we feel that he comprehends their absurdities the while, "benetted 'round with villainies," he struggles manfully with Claudius, his "mighty opposite."

In a study of *Hamlet*, Jean S. Calhoun has revealed the differing circumferences of vision and action among its characters: "*Hamlet* displays a hierarchy of subjectively identified scenes, ranging from the personal and private, through the civic and national, to the 'undiscovered country' beyond the earth. The many circumferences radiate concentrically from the characters' actions and intentions to encompass ever wider scenes, until they embrace the ultimate possible scene of human action—the eternal, cosmic, or divine scene."[14] Tragic awareness, I have noted, is inseparable from seeing any creation in nature doomed to disaster before "time's battering ram." The gravediggers do see the skull, but they slight the sad mutations of which it tells. Their vision is narrowly that of the radically comic. The immediate business of this earth also bounds the horizons (in different ways) of Claudius and Gertrude, of Polonius and his young, of Rosencrantz and Guildenstern, of Fortinbras, and of all the other characters except Horatio and Hamlet. The former wisely considers nothing "too curiously," is not "fortune's slave." Hamlet, however, knows too well that there "are more things in heaven and earth, Horatio, than are dreamt of in your philosophy." He so readily voyages through any "strange seas of thought unknown" that his name has become almost synonymous with the tragic contemplative spirit of modern man. He knows the full range of "this quintessence of dust" that with its large "discourse of reason" "looking before and after" scans the heavens yet may finally stop a bunghole. We never see him free of grief and only at the beginning without the burden of the ghost's charge to avenge his beloved father's death, a charge made exceedingly difficult because he is commanded to leave his adulterous mother to heaven and to taint not his mind (as Laertes taints his in seeking blind vengeance for his father's death). Moreover, as a rational man he must first prove the validity of the visitor from another world. Yet there are a few speeches with his university friends and with the players, as well as Ophelia's portrait of him as "th' expectancy and rose of the fair state" before the evil days came nigh, to suggest that Hamlet then knew mirth and laughter—that he keeps a submerged sense of the freely comic.

Perhaps a final word on the comic in *Hamlet* will have more meaning if I first glance at comic strains in some other tragedies, even at the risk of saying things long stock.

Everyone remembers the comic characters in *Romeo and Juliet*. Its Nurse is a richly farcical piece of genre painting, deliciously amusing in gabbing on quite heedless of the comic gap between the actualities of her situation at the

moment and her ambling patter. Old Capulet appears ironically kin to his vulgar servant in his own comic unaware-
ness of the irrelevancy of his domestic chatter to the actual
nature of the occasions when we hear it. He foreshadows
Polonius. Mercutio is a superb comedian, acutely aware
of the absurd aspect of the vulgar Nurse, of lovesick
Romeo, and of everything else (even Queen Mab). His
merry, sportive wit plays irrepressibly until fate makes
a "grave" man of him. Witty even while dying, he is
as fine-grained a comic foil for Romeo as the Nurse is
a coarse-grained one for Juliet. Puns and word-play, sometimes forced for modern tastes, illustrate in Mercutio and
in others their limited value that I at the outset remarked
upon. Bawdy or obscene speeches amuse us and help
to root the passionate love of Romeo and Juliet in the
actual world of flesh and blood. They are rightly given
a comic cast in being spoken in the main by the leading
comic characters, Mercutio and the Nurse. And for mature
tastes, they are not discordant with Juliet's candid avowals
of her love.[15]

Most readers forget the clown in *Othello*, and justly,
for his few speeches (III.i,iv) interest chiefly students who
ponder his poor "quillets" and their incidental footing
in an overwhelming pyramiding of tragic ironies.[16] And
though Iago may have in his family tree the comic Vice
of the old moralities, his actions in *Othello* are about as
far from comic as deeds can get, whatever the impact
of his sardonic wit.[17] There is nothing subtle about the
comic stature of the drunken porter in *Macbeth*, though
he has long been recognized as (ironically) more a porter
at hell's gate than he can know when he cries "Here's
a knocking indeed! If a man were porter of hell gate, he
should have old turning the key" (II.iii.1–3). His bawdy
patter about sex and liquor catapults us back into commonplace reality after the dreadful murder of Duncan. Thomas
De Quincey wrote a classic exposition of this jerk back
into everyday life that the porter effects and the almost

simultaneous heightening of our sense of the horror of the bloody deed now done. The radically comic impact of his speeches is half neutralized by the terrible tragic setting; we can scarcely attend to their comic aspect before being swiftly deflected to the awfulness of their background. When, however, the country clown in *Antony and Cleopatra* brings the queen the basket of asps and repeatedly wishes her "joy of the worm," we are freely amused not only by the comic clash in the diction, but also by the abrupt one between the exalted queen and her lowly countryman with his rustic prattle because, whatever the pity of her plight, there is little or no tragic terror about her impending end: the "stroke of death" from "the pretty worm of Nilus" will be but "as a lover's pinch / Which hurts, and is desir'd" (V.ii.298–299). Because of this lack of tragic terror in the setting, the messenger who tells of Antony's marriage to Octavia can topple Cleopatra from her throne when she rages and *"hales him up and down"* as might any common shrew. Giving Cleopatra such a comic dimension helps us to feel her "infinite variety." Akin to the radically comic moments created by the rustic and the messenger are the bawdy and witty speeches of Iras and Charmian in I.ii. Their divertingly comic impact is also unqualified by any gravely tragic setting.

Complicated, however, are many of the speeches of that sophisticated character Enobarbus before he, master ironist, is ironically caught up in the tragic web of the play to die of heartbreak as a "master-leaver and a fugitive." He can smile in admiration or amusement before the dazzling spectacle of Cleopatra in her barge, mistress of charms of "infinite variety"; he can wittily give Antony "light answers" about Fulvia's death; he can out-carouse all his fellows on Pompey's galley and out-talk them in swift and witty repartee. And he can speak with the chorus-like voice of truth itself in his vain efforts to save Antony from the folly of his courses.[18] In his witty, detached, and correctively comic comments meant to bring Antony to his senses, Enobarbus is a cousin to Lear's Fool. That supremely complex comic creation is the ultimate transmutation of the traditional court jester or licensed truth-speaker into a pivotal tool for effecting the spiritual regeneration of Lear. So profound is the tragic milieu of all the Fool's jests that our awareness of royal Lear become a "poor, weak, despised old man" is both less and more than a comic awareness because totally devoid of the irresponsible playfulness in the trade wit of the professional court jester and freighted with the sympathy of a devoted servant. His speeches strike with a correctively comic impact, become wittily mordant and ironic; yet we never doubt that they spring from love of his master as they stab at his folly. And they somehow simultaneously nurture our sense of ineffable pity for the mighty monarch being stripped down to the "poor, barren, forked animal" that "unaccommodated man" is in truth. The wisely mad fool brings the foolish king gone mad to full awareness of his common humanity. This ironic turnabout reminds us anew that we make but puny human distinctions when in the ultimate junctures of life we see anything as exclusively comic or exclusively tragic. In the topsy-turvy days of our subsiding century the point acquires fresh meaning as major dramatists refuse to separate the farcical from the tragic.[19]

Comic materials in the great tragedies that I have glanced at effect the spread if not the depth of the vision that distinguishes them.[20] Rising within the extant moment from an essentially playful angle on the radical contrast between the existential facts and their conventional representations, comic vision has as its inevitable complement the grave and long-time point of view that sees facts and forms woven into the web of life in which each of us in his fashion is fatally caught to fill his little niche in the eternal realm of the truth.[21] No play has given modern sensibility so adequate an awareness of this dual nature of the human lot as has *Hamlet*. Many readings of it have warped it by concentrating too exclusively upon the predicament of its protagonist. Well might Coleridge and his descendants have remembered that for Shakespeare and his motley audience the play was the primary thing—the play in all its fullness. Its story was a not unfamiliar one of deferred revenge for the murder of a beloved father, yet revenge not reprehensibly delayed, as is proved by the laudation of the prince both by Horatio and Fortinbras at the finish. The famous soliloquies first explicate Hamlet's predicament and help make plausible in the playhouse his deferred revenge—all that dramatic illusion really requires.[22] Shortsighted scrutiny of them in the study, as if they were parts of a dramatic poem rather than of a poetic drama, has wrongly made Hamlet for many the type par excellence of an irresolute man, "sicklied o'er with the pale cast of thought," enfeebled of will, and unable to act. Those soliloquies do classically voice the tragic outlook on life. In them Hamlet does take the long view of human affairs, see what an unweeded garden this world in truth is, and decry "the slings and arrows of outrageous fortune." Yet he also wrestles manfully with a "mighty opposite" though "benetted 'round with villainies."[23] So caught, he understandably finds it impossible to take playfully the absurdities of life as the extant moment discloses them for free laughter. When we juxtapose Hamlet's expressions about life to Falstaff's way with it, we get a clearcut view of the two complementary angles on it. Yet within *Hamlet* are richly comic moments that give the audience the two angles within one play. The gravediggers heedlessly tossing skulls are like Falstaff recruiting cannon fodder—all laugh irresponsibly at the basic absurdity of the human condition. Without the gravediggers and Polonius and Osric, the tragic vision of the play that sweeps over heaven and earth would lack roundness and resonance and the play would falsify the full truth.

CHAPTER VII

EPILOGUE

Today we are so aware of the irrational in life as it batters all the traditional ramparts of civilization that we understandably feel little liberty to catch a freely comic slant on existence, and laugh. In our distracted days the comic and the tragic as Shakespeare presents them have often crossed to yield strange fruit in the drama. An underlying satiric impulse of anger and disgust gives much of it a bitter taste. Plot and character vanish in plays wherein symbolic puppets voice themes of alienation and hopelessness. In echoing our confusion and desperation since Auschwitz and Hiroshima, Beckett, Ionesco, and their followers inevitably come home to our disillusioned bosoms as many of their antecedents now do not. Before some plays in our age of over-kill we weep and wryly smile almost simultaneously—when we have not become inured to both laughter and tears. Often pity and terror are undercut by revulsion and despair; free laughter is stifled; and the traditionally comic and tragic are stymied by cosmic irony.

David Worcester has written discerningly that "laughter and tears are reconciled in irony; it brings laughter to tragedy and tears to comedy," "acts as a counterpoise to the emotions raised by either tragedy or comedy," and "furnishes an alternative scale of values which prevents the spectator from being altogether carried away by sympathy with the actors." It "tends to neutralize all passions and to turn all men into spectators of the human comedy. Up to a point, this is a useful function. Irony delights in the collision of opposites. When the mind is paralyzed by conflicting drives, irony offers a way of escaping from the conflict and rising above it. The reason is saved from the shattering effect of divergent commands, and the mind regains its equilibrium."[1] Used for such rational ends—to bring the spirit poise and freedom from the tyranny of things and humble it by enlarging its awareness of the "unsimple truth"—irony is an invaluable base for the life of reason. But, as Worcester points out, in the habitual ironist the springs of action dry up, "for in the nightmare world of relativity nothing is worth doing, *all things considered....* The inveterate ironist escapes from paralysis of the mind only to fall a victim to paralysis of the will."[2] Divorced from genuine humor and eventual action in the world of affairs (as it was not in such a master of it as Chaucer), irony becomes cosmic irony such as nurtures the profound cultural malaise that afflicts the world today.

Cosmic irony "is the satire of frustration, uttered by men who believe that however high man's aspirations and calculations may reach, there is always a still higher, unattainable level of knowledge, in the light of which those aspirations and calculations must become stultified and abortive."[3] Cosmic irony grew apace in the nineteenth century as expanding science and scholarship made men aware of more and more irreconcilable clashes between new knowledge and inherited forms for ordering experience. As science in our revolutionary century has split the atom and kept multiplying anew our awareness of ironic clashes between contradictory facts in all areas of human activity, the dangerously negative side of irony has been exposed and become dominant in our sensibility.

The cosmic "irony of the modern hero serves no ulterior purpose and reveals no creative thought. It is irony for its own sake; a manner worn as a protective garment by a dissociated and neurotic personality. No condemnation is intended. To the extent that the modern world has destroyed our sources of sublimation and reduced us all to dissociated and neurotic personalities, we are happy to grasp at irony in order to preserve our sanity."[4] "A world in which everything is ironical is a neurotic and unhappy place."[5] "Besides *tedium vitae* and the revolt against God, a third theme for cosmic irony is the vision of earth as a speck of dust,"[6] intensified as the common man learns that he is millions of light years away from vast objects in space that make his planet a puny mite in the scheme of things entire.

Yet, as Worcester asked a generation ago, need cosmic irony overwhelm us? "A fact is admittedly right and an idea is usually wrong, but neither one can have meaning without the other. To dare to create may be to risk making a fool of oneself; but if Horace and Lucian and Chaucer and Rabelais and Swift were not above making fools of themselves, what is there to fear?"[7] Wise and courageous men with humor and discipline have always risen above the inevitable irony of things to enlightened action among them. Rational life above the hurly-burly of man-made objects is not impossible today, only exceedingly difficult. But when was it easy? The life of reason may be a flying goal for most of us much of the time. But what other goal is truly worth pursuing?

The comic and the tragic aspects of life are but the obverse and reverse of a totality that appears a blind surd at bottom, an irrational flux. Yet over long time that flux has paradoxically mothered values that rational men have cherished, however small the pittance of reason allowed them by Swift. When we take the long view life may often seem a tale told by an idiot. Certainly it is today increasingly full of sound and fury. But "it is far from signifying nothing."[8] It signifies all we for certain have. And "midmost the beating of the steely sea" we must build whatever "shadowy isle of bliss" we are to be assured of. Even in their grim view of the truth *Othello*, *Macbeth*, and *Lear* achieve such freedom as wisdom long ago assured us the truth brings when unflinchingly known. All is not darkness in *Lear* or in life no matter how much some men today distort both to make them appear so. Jan Kott's fashionable dark glasses hardly help us to see Shakespeare plain.[9] Cordelia, Kent, and the Fool have as firm a footing in the realm of truth as have Goneril, Regan, and Edmund. Before Lear loses the world in agony, he has gained something more precious. And always a free comic eye can find with Falstaff momentary delight, itself a part of the full truth as much as any sorrow. "An aimless joy is a pure joy."[10] Falstaff complements Hamlet. Benedick and Beatrice and Rosalind and Viola complement both of them. And Prospero gives perspective on all.

For, as we have earlier heard Santayana declare, "life is free play fundamentally."[11] A free mind knows that "it is no interruption to experience to master experience, as tragedy aspires to do; nor is it an interruption to sink into its episodes and render them consummate, which is the trick of comedy."[12] "Free life has the spirit of comedy. It rejoices in the seasonable beauty of each new thing, and laughs at its decay, covets no possessions, demands no agreement, and strives to sustain nothing in being except a gallant spirit of courage and truth, as each fresh adventure may renew it."[13] "The happy presence of reason in human life is perhaps better exemplified in comedy than in tragedy. In comedy we see no terrible sub-human or super-human fatality to render reason vain. Reason therefore can make its little runs and show its comic contradictions and clever solutions without disturbing the sound vegetative substance and free flowerings of human society. In comedy we laugh at our foolish errors, correct them with a word, and know no reason why we shouldn't be happy ever after."[14]

So it is in Shakespearean comedy; but so it is not today in "black comedy," in the "theatre of the absurd," "of revolt," "of protest and paradox."[15] There lonely and alienated man feels lost in a world that is but a speck in an immeasurable universe not molded after his heart's desire. When juxtaposed to that fathomless creation, the "minute motion and pullulation in the earth's crust of which human affairs are a portion"[16] seems absurd indeed. But the absurdity evokes little free and merry laughter such as the unplumbed spectacle yielded in simpler days, perhaps partly because man today feels less assured of benevolent deities behind the scenes and more enmeshed by unnerving cosmic irony. Free laughter at the radical absurdity of things has come from men with an unimpeded sense of it. Now the upshot is often revolt against life itself in all its fundamental absurdity.[17] What is absurd is what is at odds with reason; and reason is a vital and but a human harmony, always in precarious equilibrium, now lost, now found, between inner impulses and the external forces that assault the individual consciousness, between action and renunciation.[18] Even the most absurd drama of the "absurd" appeals to it at least implicitly. And the freely comic is itself undermined if reason with her seasoned conventions that are essential for any sustained life is long violated or renounced.[19]

Yet, as Santayana well knew, "our logical thoughts dominate experience only as the parallels and meridians make a checker-board of the sea. They guide our voyage without controlling the waves, which toss for ever in spite of our ability to ride over them to our chosen ends. Sanity is a madness put to good uses; waking life is a dream controlled."[20] Juxtaposed to those tossing, unplumbed waves, our "logical thoughts" of course appear "to reason most absurd"—ridiculous to the comic eye. But are those "parallels and meridians" vain if they "guide our voyage" and we remember that "man was not made to understand the world, but to live in it"?[21] Nearly lost in it now for all his vaunted "progress", man, were he not "sore distracted" by the deluge of things that he and his machines multiply often without rhyme or reason, and were he truly humble before his lot in nature, might capture again some of the free laughter in Shakespeare's comic creations. His pivotal experiences in life remain ours—birth and inevitable death after the struggle for happiness during our strange interlude "here, upon this bank and shoal of time." Nor do drugs, organ transplants, and genetic engineering promise soon to change them.

Shakespeare wrote in times full of troubles, many not ours, but most the abiding lot of "our proud and angry dust." The difference between Shakespeare's times and ours "may perhaps be summed up by saying that Shakespeare's age was breaking into chaos, while our age is trying to turn chaos into order."[22] Yet his tragedy faced destiny with neither a bang nor a whimper and his comedy rose free of confusion and despair in humorous, unfettered laughter at the sheer absurdity of the passing spectacle. Scholars preserve his texts, however violated when the plays are staged as "far out" interpretations of the originals.[23] Students who remember Restoration manglings of the plays can take present treatments in perspective, confident that the originals will survive the bias of a time when many men, despairing of reason, have reverted to jungle morality. Often we scrap traditional values, forms, and conventions for mishmashes that sensationalize sex and violence. Perhaps we do so inevitably as new knowledge and power pile up everywhere more swiftly than confused men, who know that one of them could push buttons and destroy every living thing, can digest all for rational life.

Half a century ago Santayana wrote with prescience:

Civilisation is perhaps approaching one of those long winters that overtake it from time to time. A flood of barbarism from below may soon level all the fair works of our Christian ancestors, as another flood two thousand years ago levelled those of the ancients. Romantic Christendom—picturesque, passionate, unhappy episode—may be coming to an end. Such a catastrophe would be no reason for despair. Nothing lasts for ever; but the elasticity of life is wonderful, and even if the world lost its memory it could not lose its youth. Under the deluge, and watered by it, seeds of all sorts would survive against the time to come, even if what might eventually spring from them, under the new circumstances, should wear a strange aspect. In a certain measure, and unintentionally, both this destruction and this restoration have already occurred in America. There is much forgetfulness, much callow disrespect for what is past or alien; but there is a fund of vigour, goodness, and hope such as no nation ever possessed before. In what sometimes looks like American greediness and jostling for the front place, all is love of achievement, nothing is unkindness; it is a fearless people, and free from malice, as you might see in their eyes and gestures, even if their conduct did not prove it. This soil is propitious to every seed, and tares must needs grow in it; but why should it not also breed clear thinking, honest judgement, and rational happiness? These things are indeed not necessary to existence, and without them America might long remain rich and populous like many a barbarous land in the past; but in that case its existence would be hounded, like theirs, by falsity and remorse. May Heaven avert the omen, and make the new world a better world than the old! In the classical and romantic tradition of Europe, love, of which there was very little, was supposed to be kindled by beauty, of which there was a great deal: perhaps moral chemistry may be able to reverse this operation, and in the future and in America it may breed beauty out of love.[24]

Santayana's words now ring for Americans with sad ironies. Malice and unkindness deplete the inherited fund of "vigour, goodness, and hope." Some cry that the American dream has turned into a nightmare. Crime and violence mount in the country—over the world. Leaders have been assassinated. Advertising idiocies and cheap sensationalism in the arts corrupt integrity and taste. Race tensions tear the fabric of the social order from the jungles of decaying cities to Main Street as greedy waste-makers plunder and pollute limited natural resources. In schools and universities (not only in America) where "clear thinking" and "honest judgement" should be nurtured for "rational happiness," strikes, violent protests, and drug addiction threaten the fountain of rational life. Distant and divisive wars have drained America of precious lives and billions of dollars direly needed at home. What will it profit men if they gain the moon and lose the good earth? And all the while the arms race in weapons unimaginably terrible plunges the world toward doomsday. One might understandably cry that ours is no time for comedy. Yet laugh we must, for the other "way madness lies."

Santayana described the life of reason early in his career—1905–1906. He died in 1952, half a dozen years after the atomic bomb catapulted us into the age of overkill, in which the earth as the mother of us all could indeed not "last for ever." It could "lose its youth." We could make it again the lifeless cinder in space it once was. The discords that today sound over the whole globe—not just in America—demand "clear thinking" and "honest judgement" if the revolutions wrought by Marx, Einstein, Freud, and their associates are to fructify in a new synthesis—in "rational happiness." Mere permissiveness is hardly enough, though a "now" generation appears to think so. Life no more ends at thirty than it begins at forty. Our hedonistic cult of sensational life in the moment is rebuked by Santayana's best known epigram: "Those who cannot remember the past are condemned to repeat it."[25] Rational life is inevitably an individual discipline, traditionally spread over three score and ten years, and sustained by some measure of political order, sooner or later, it now appears, an international one, direly needed in a turbulent world that swift communication has, willy-nilly, united. Perhaps the rampant irrationalities of our time in almost all spheres, public and personal, cannot be controlled by any "moral chemistry." Should extinction be ahead for technetronic man who races into space while millions of his brothers still starve, die of curable diseases, "liquidate" one another in wars or non-wars, and devastate and defile the earth as they promiscuously multiply toward famine upon it, the plays of Shakespeare will serve as a house of humane refuge as that man deservedly disappears. Should technetronic man be destined to survive his current woes and evolve into a new species under the sun that will transcend the humanity of the plays, they will remain to tell any curious creatures to come what man long was before "tragic" and "comic" became cultural fossils. Even now, the comic strains in Shakespeare are an oasis for the life of reason so beseiged that it often seems a mere will-o'-the-wisp, not a steady beacon light, to "organization men" who in an affluent society (with "poverty pockets") form a lonely crowd making a waste land, and sheltered by missiles, anti-missiles, and hydrogen bombs for a final fire next time.

In our depressing days Falstaff, Viola, and their companions are old friends worth keeping. They know freedom of spirit, and, as Santayana reminds us, "free spirit lets the dead bury their dead, and takes no thought for the morrow; and it redeems the labouring world by bringing joy into it."[26] "A free mind, like a creative imagination, rejoices at the harmonies it can find or make between man and nature; and, where it finds none, it solves the conflict so far as it may and then notes and endures it with a shudder."[27] As Orwell's 1984 approaches we have cause aplenty for shudders. But the "easier attitudes which seem more frivolous are at bottom infinitely more spiritual and profound than the tense attitudes; they are nearer to understanding and to renunciation; they are nearer to the cross."[28] If a man—as we have already heard Santayana declare—"aspires to shed as much as possible the delusions of earthly passion, and to look at things joyfully and unselfishly, ... it is not because he feels no weight of affliction, but precisely because he feels its weight to the full, and how final it is."[29]

I turn at the end to Santayana; he looked long and deep into the abyss, yet wrote *The Life of Reason* and infused almost all his pages with wit, humor, and wisdom.[30] He could focus precisely the predicament of reason: "That life is worth living is the most necessary of assumptions and, were it not assumed, the most impossible of conclusions."[31] Again, the "knowledge that existence can manifest but cannot retain the good reconciles us at once to living and to dying."[32] But he could also declare that "nature, in denying us perennial youth, has at least invited us to become unselfish and noble."[33] Again, "what a despicable creature must a man be and how sunk below the level of the most barbaric virtue, if he cannot bear to live for his children, for his art, or for country!"[34]

My last quotation from Santayana is the last paragraph of the Preface to his *Realms of Being:*

In confessing that I have merely touched the hem of nature's garment, I feel that virtue from her has passed into me, and made me whole. There is no more bewitching moment in childhood than when the boy, to whom someone is slyly propounding some absurdity, suddenly looks up and smiles. The brat has understood. A thin deception was being practised on him, in hope that he might not be deceived, but by deriding it might prove he had attained to a man's stature and a man's wit. It was but banter prompted by love. So with this thin deception practised upon me by nature. The great Sphinx in posing her riddle and looking so threatening and mysterious is secretly hoping that I may laugh. She is not a riddle but a fact; the words she whispers are not oracles but prattle. Why take her residual silence, which is inevitable, for a challenge or a menace? She does not know how to speak more plainly. Her secret is as great a secret to herself as to me. If I perceive it, and laugh, instantly she draws in her claws. A tremor runs through her enigmatical body; and if she were not of stone she would embrace her boyish discoverer, and yield herself to him altogether. It is so simple to exist, to be what one is for no reason, to engulf all questions and answers in the rush of being that sustains them. Henceforth nature and spirit can play together like mother and child, each marvelously pleasant to the other, yet deeply unintelligible; for as she created him she knew not how, merely by smiling in her dreams, so in awaking and smiling back he somehow understands her; at least he is all the understanding she has of herself.[35]

Might not Shakespeare have smiled understandingly before such humor and wisdom about the abiding absurdity and mystery of things?

Must man now fail in his pursuit of a life of reason just when his sphinx-like mother is yielding to him such knowledge of her hidden ways as already frees him from much pain and most drudgery? Why should her only creation *capax rationis* not turn the atom he has split to his rational happiness rather than to the destruction of himself and his good earth?

In their way with the comic—in their humor and wisdom that transcend crippling cosmic irony—Shakespeare and Santayana can sustain men who, "beleaguered by . . . / Negation and despair" as never before, would "show an affirming flame."[36]

NOTES

Chapter I

[1]"Richter remarked with reason, 'Definitions of the comic serve the sole purpose of being themselves comic' " (David Worcester, *The Art of Satire* [Cambridge, Mass., 1940], p. 10).

[2]*Every Man in his Humour*, Prologue, ll. 21–24, in *Ben Jonson*, ed. C. H. Herford and Percy Simpson, III (Oxford, 1927), 303.

[3]*Every Man out of his Humour*, Prologue, ll. 17–20, in *Ben Jonson*, III, 428–429.

[4]*Every Man out of his Humour*, III.vi.207–209, in *Ben Jonson*, III, 515.

[5]Preface to *Tartuffe*, in *Œuvres de Molière*, ed. Eugène Despois and Paul Mesnard (Paris, n. d.), IV, 377.

[6]*An Essay on Comedy and the Uses of the Comic Spirit*, ed. Lane Cooper (Ithaca, N. Y., 1956).

[7]*Laughter: An Essay on the Meaning of the Comic*, trans. Cloudesley Brereton and Fred Rothwell (New York, 1928), p. 136. Bergson grounds the comic on " 'something mechanical encrusted upon the living' " (p. 49). "The comic is that side of a person which reveals his likeness to a thing, that aspect of human events which, through its peculiar inelasticity, conveys the impression of pure mechanism, of automatism, of movement without life. Consequently it expresses an individual or collective imperfection which calls for an immediate corrective. This corrective is laughter, a social gesture that singles out and represses a special kind of absent-mindedness in men and in events" (pp. 87–88). The view of the comic set forth in this chapter grounds it upon the absurd and laughable contrast between natural

fact and encrusting convention; it stresses a playful spirit and point of view in time as essential for catching the comic dimension of anything in nature; and it does not see the comic as primarily corrective.

[8]See the persuasive argument in Thomas H. Fujimura's *The Restoration Comedy of Wit* (Princeton, N. J., 1952).

[9]Preface to *L'Enfant Prodigue*, in *Œuvres Complètes* (Paris, 1877), III, 444.

[10]Hobbes, *Leviathan*, ed. Michael Oakeshott (Oxford, 1960), p. 36.

[11]"Now to tell you in plain woordes what laughter is, how it stirreth and occupieth the whole body, how it altereth the countenaunce, and sodainly brasteth out that we cannot kepe it in, let some mery man, on Goddes name, take this matter in hande. For it passeth my cunninge, and I thynke euen thei that can best moue laughter would rather laugh merily when suche a question is put furthe, then geue aunswere earnestly, what, and how laughter is in deede" (Thomas Wilson, *The Arte of Rhetorique*, in *Sixteenth-Century English Prose*, ed. Karl J. Holzknecht [New York, 1954], p. 159). The psychologists, not markedly "mery men," sometimes move us to laughter by their explanations that we wish they would explain; still, they and the physiologists are the men to have the final say about a subject as deep as existence. I do not claim to have weighed all their many and often divergent explanations.

[12]"When I Went to the Circus—," in *The Complete Poems*, ed. Vivian de Sola Pinto and Warren Roberts (New York, 1964), I, 446. All parents can recount instances of their children puncturing adult pretenses by questions or comments more or less amusing in pointing to facts or things obscured by the conventions of adult life. For children the past has not become a burden and the future an anxiety; hence they can attend to the immediate, to whatever pops into their consciousness, with a freedom denied grownups to whom disillusionment has not brought detachment enough to free them for catching in the flying moment its disclosure of the absurdity of the conventional. "The immediate is what nobody sees, because convention and reflection turn existence, as soon as they can, into ideas; a man who discloses the immediate seems profound, yet his depth is nothing but innocence recovered and a sort of intellectual abstention" (Santayana, *The Life of Reason or the Phases of Human Progress*, 2nd ed. [New York, 1924], I [*Reason in Common Sense*], 15).

[13]The several quotations are from Santayana, *Soliloquies in England and Later Soliloquies* (New York, 1923), pp. 135–136.

[14]I would distinguish between the comic and the tragic on the one hand and comedy and tragedy on the other: the latter are complex art structures, whether dramatic or not, for which the comic and tragic as I construe them are the building stones. My focus falls on such

stones as Shakespeare used in his comedies, not upon his architectonics, though I often remark on his edifices and hope not to obscure
them.

¹⁵*Soliloquies,* pp. 141–142, 142, 144.

¹⁶Santayana, *Obiter Scripta* (New York, 1936), p. 170.

¹⁷*Poems and Dramas,* ed. Geoffrey Bullough (New York, 1945), II,
136.

¹⁸*Soliloquies,* pp. 144, 132, 137.

¹⁹That "everything in nature is lyrical in its ideal essence" is not
my primary interest. Suffice to say that the lyrical can forget the noose
that tethers it to existence and to truth as the comic and the tragic
cannot. The end for the lyrical is pure and untroubled contemplation
of essence, illustrated or not by existence in that segment of being
that we call the truth. The truth of things did stir Lucretius to great
lyrical strains; but the lyrical poet usually hymns freely his heart's
desire—fancy bred more in his heart than in his head. Proust spoke
for the lyrical outlook of spirit when he wrote: "what *happens* in a
man's life is without interest, and to the scholar and the artist seems
merely accidental, so long as it is stripped of those feelings which
are the constituents of poetry" *(Jean Santeuil,* trans. Gerard Hopkins
[New York, 1956], p. 590). The lyrical is classically illustrated by Shakespeare's Sonnets though many of them are pervaded by a tragic sense
of the transience of all things.

²⁰Santayana is writing of Dickens as a master of comedy comparable
"to the very greatest comic poets, to Shakespeare or to Aristophanes"
(Soliloquies, p. 68); hence I think his observations equally relevant to
my subject. "In seeing Dickens as an outstanding example of uncontaminated naturalism, Santayana also takes him as the prototype of
all comedy. Comedy sees things externally, as brute occurrences in
nature which have no necessary reason for being. The existence of
anything is, as the existentialists would say, 'absurd'—we can never
prove deductively that anything must or must not be. Comedy cuts
beneath convention in order to show the absurdity of everything, in
order to reduce every existent to its fundamental materiality. Comedy
requires courage, and is usually cruel. Dickens had the courage, but
not the cruelty. Santayana praises him for combining naturalistic
insight with universal kindness which tempers his savage strokes and
allows the reader to enjoy the comic spectacle in which he is himself
a participant" (Irving Singer, editing Santayana, *Essays in Literary
Criticism* [New York, 1956], pp. xv–xvi). Shakespeare, too, tempers
the severity of pure comedy in various ways, as will be seen.

²¹Stephen Spender quotes W. H. Auden on "the poet" as he
apprehends truth: "the tragic, at its greatest, is always funny: '*enter*

Lear with Cordelia in his arms. Lear: Howl, howl, howl!' Or that scene in *War and Peace*, where Pierre rushes into the burning building to save a baby and the baby turns and bites him" *(World Within World* [London, 1951], p. 62). The heroic and the tragic in art are, after all, but man-made abstractions from the rushing welter of events with which they collide ridiculously if we suddenly shift our point of view—see a baby as it is in *actual* life. Our tragic postures when exalted and sustained invite the comic eye; witness the invitation that the heroically tragic constantly offers to parody and burlesque.

²²This, I think, is the truth that Walpole struck at.

²³Is it not the measure of Charlie Chaplin's stature that he is not a clown of this sort? And of Marcel Marceau's power as a pantominist?

²⁴Santayana, *Soliloquies*, pp. 66–70.

²⁵Chekhov projects character dishabille in a dual and not dissimilar way, but with his own subtle accent on muted strings; hence the continual argument as to whether his plays are to be acted as comedies or as tragedies—though he significantly wished them acted as comedies. Perhaps for most sensibility today the emphasis in his particular amalgam of the tragic and the comic falls upon facts that (to reorder Santayana's phrase), "however absurd outwardly, are always serious inwardly."

²⁶Louis Cazamian reminds us that humor is not necessarily genial in its sufferance, though usually so in England. See *The Development of English Humor* (Durham, N. C., 1952). Sardonic humor is, I think, humor crossed by the hotly satiric and, perhaps, the sarcastic, which is in turn the splenetically ironic.

²⁷Santayana, *Soliloquies*, p. 141.

²⁸I introduce the term "festive" with a bow to C. L. Barber's valuable study, *Shakespeare's Festive Comedy* (Princeton, N. J., 1959). Barber prefers "festive" to "romantic" as an epithet for the comedies that culminate with *Twelfth Night:* "festive" focuses the folk base that he thinks is vital in such Shakespearean comedies. Barber, Northrop Frye ("The Argument of Comedy," in *English Institute Essays, 1948,* ed. D. A. Robertson, Jr. [New York, 1949]), and Janet Spens (*An Essay on Shakespeare's Relation to Tradition* [Oxford, 1916]) hold that "medieval folk-festivals, based on ritual, were a major influence on Shakespeare's Comedies" (E. M. W. Tillyard, *Shakespeare's Early Comedies* [London, 1965], p. 29). Tillyard dissents: "To have any paramount significance, to be worth serious distinction from the general instinct for periodical jollification, these festivals must remain what they once were: pieces of ritual intended to lead to practical results. I am most doubtful of their so remaining in the age of Chaucer and feel certain that they did not by the time of Shakespeare. They served well enough as means

162

of periodical amusement; they were still part of life; but as applied to literature they are too generalized in significance to help in our understanding of it" (p. 29). My recognition of a play instinct as fundamental in the comic is relevant to a "festival" strain in it. I have chosen to keep the traditional adjective "romantic" partly because in the chapters ahead my overall angle on the comic invites its retention.

[29]*The New York Times,* June 1, 1958, Section II, p. 3.

[30]Quoted in Martin Esslin, *The Theatre of the Absurd* (Garden City, N. Y., 1961), p. 101.

[31]Jan Kott, *Shakespeare Our Contemporary* (Garden City, N. Y., 1964). See above, p. 150, and below, pp. 181–182.

[32]Eric Bentley authoritatively informs me that the phrase, although an echo of much comment on farce today, is dubiously Brecht's.

[33]"Nature is innocent, and so are all her impulses and moods when taken in isolation; it is only on meeting that they blush" (Santayana, *The Life of Reason,* revised by the author in collaboration with Daniel Cory [New York, 1954], p. 363). "Moral judgments and conflicts are possible only in the mind that represents many interests synthetically: in nature, where primary impulses collide, all conflict is physical and all will innocent" (p. 321).

[34]Santayana, *Soliloquies,* p. 97.

[35]Willard Farnham has revealed the relevant glorification of the fool in the Middle Ages as it was assimilated by Shakespeare ("The Medieval Comic Spirit in the English Renaissance," in *Joseph Quincy Adams Memorial Studies,* ed. James G. McManaway, Giles E. Dawson, and Edwin E. Willoughby [Washington, D. C., 1948], pp. 429–437).

[36]William Roper, *The Life of Syr Thomas More,* in *Sixteenth-Century English Prose,* p. 183.

[37]*Measure for Measure,* II.ii.117–122.

[38]Charles Lamb wrote: "I cannot divest me of an unseasonable disposition to levity upon the most awful occasions" (*The Works of Charles and Mary Lamb,* ed. Thomas Hutchinson [London, n. d.], I, 772). Lamb could jest about his six-weeks confinement to a madhouse and see the absurd aspects of christenings, weddings, and even funerals. A funeral is sad for those who have loved the deceased, less so for his doctor and undertaker, and a matter of total indifference for nearly everybody else—even of high satisfaction for his enemies. In *The Playboy of the Western World* Synge sports delightfully with patricide for radically comic effects. Point of view is basic for catching the comic dimension of anything.

[39]"The child is not just the father of man [*sic*], but his sibling, too, in that he survives alongside the adult, and as his Siamese twin. There are levels of playful, libidinous unreality in all of us" (Jonathan Miller,

"Another Wonderland," in *The New·York Times Book Review,* May 7, 1967, Part II, p. 1).

[40]These attributes are seen as essential in the conception of humor that pervades Cazamian's *The Development of English Humor.*

[41]Screeners of Mau Mau reported: " 'Ridicule's our strongest weapon.' " The screeners made the accused natives "feel fools—and that's far more effective than violence. In the end, nearly all of them confess." "A second woman, dressed in old-style Kikuyu goatskins, beads and ear ornaments, sat on the ground before them and denied everything. She'd never even heard of Mau Mau. The screeners were laughing themselves silly. They knew the old woman had taken two Mau Mau oaths at least, and her vehement denials tickled them to death" (Elsbeth Huxley, "What Life is Like for a Settler in Kenya," in *The New York Times Magazine,* June 6, 1954, p. 60).

[42]Worcester, *The Art of Satire,* p. 16.

[43]Revealing is George Sherburn's characterization of Goldsmith as "too hard-headed to be a thorough sentimentalist, and too sympathetic to be an outright satirist" (*A Literary History of England,* ed. Albert C. Baugh [New York, 1948], p. 1062). My thoughts about the satiric owe not a little to Gilbert Highet.

[44]I have been seeking concepts of the comic, the humorous, and the satiric that would signify for various art forms. Mediums, of course, radically condition forms; I would simply keep my central terms relevant, for example, to aspects of Mozart and Prokofiev, of Hogarth and Goya, of Daumier and Franz Hals and Peter Brueghel—as well as Shakespeare. And of course in playhouse drama various physical media determine any welding of the comic, the humorous, the satiric, and any other ingredients in a hundred ways with which the dramatist and critic must reckon.

[45]Worcester, *The Art of Satire,* p. 165.

[46]Ibid., 81.

[47]Ibid., 75–76.

[48]G. G. Sedgwick, *Of Irony: Especially in Drama* (Toronto, 1948), p. 49.

[49]Worcester, *The Art of Satire,* p. 76. See above, pp. 147–149, and below, p. 181.

[50]Worcester neatly writes: "To Freud, the comic is an anti-social impulse that sneaks past the 'censor' in disguise; once in the conscious mind, it sheds its lamb's clothing. The accumulated psychic energy finds no object to meet, and explodes as laughter" (p. 33). Freud's sustained study, "Wit and Its Relation to the Unconscious," is capped by the familiar formula: "It has seemed to us that the pleasure of wit originates from an *economy of expenditure in inhibition,* of the comic from an *economy of expenditure in thought,* and of humor from an

psychic apparatus derive pleasure from economy. All three present methods strive to bring back from the psychic activity a pleasure which has really been lost in the development of this activity. For the euphoria which we are thus striving to obtain is nothing but the state of a bygone time, in which we were wont to defray our psychic work with slight expenditure. It is the state of our childhood in which we did not know the comic, were incapable of wit, and did not need humor to make us happy" (*The Basic Writings of Sigmund Freud*, trans. and ed. A. A. Brill [New York, 1938], p. 803).

⁵¹Sidney, *The Complete Works*, ed. Albert Feuillerat (Cambridge, 1922–1926), I, 373.

⁵²Santayana, *The Sense of Beauty* (New York, 1896), pp. 250–252.

⁵³Puns have been repeatedly and variously classified. See Redmond L. O'Hanlon, "Shakespeare's Puns," in *The Shakespeare Newsletter*, March–April, 1952, p. 15. Understanding a pun loosely as "merely . . . a conscious play on words," O'Hanlon recognizes more than three thousand in Shakespeare. He classifies (with illustrations and percentages) puns as follows: "double entendre," "alliterative," "homonymous," "throwback," "holdover," "paradox," "break-up," "malaprop," "reverse," "punctuational," and "pronunciational." A double-headed homonymous pun with a comic impact (and a wry twist because of context) must illustrate the lot for us: when Polonius declares, "I did enact Julius Cæsar; I was kill'd i' th' Capitol; Brutus kill'd me," Hamlet retorts, "It was a brute part of him to kill so capital a calf there" (III.ii.108–111). Kenneth Muir has discussed the serious puns in Shakespeare with specific reference to *Macbeth* and found them contributing greatly to the dramatic and poetic effect of the play: "First, puns—and especially hidden puns—provide . . . an illogical reinforcement of the logical sequence of the thought, so that the poetic statement strikes us almost as a remembrance—as Keats said that poetry should do. Secondly, such puns often link together unrelated imagery and act as solvents for mixed metaphors. Thirdly, they make the listener aware of a complex of ideas which enrich the total statement, even though they do not come into full consciousness. Fourthly, they seem to shoot out roots in all directions, so that the poetry is firmly based on reality—a reality which is nothing less, if nothing more, than the sum total of experience" ("The Uncomic Pun," *Cambridge Journal*, III, 483). I would merely stress the comic pun as attesting the sportive play of bounding animal life that overflows in verbal exuberance to net as much absurdity as may be within a minimum of linguistic movement.

⁵⁴Lamb, *Works*, I, 792.

⁵⁵The comic as arising from a radical contrast between the "normal" or expected and the "abnormal" or unexpected is nicely illustrated

when Mary McCarthy writes that Venice " 'is another world,' people say, noting chiefly the absence of the automobile. And Venice *is* another world, a palpable fiction, in which the unexpected occurs with regularity; that is why it hovers on the brink of humor.

"A prominent nobleman this fall, rushing to the sickbed of a friend, slipped getting into his motorboat and fell into the Grand Canal. All Venice laughed. But if the count had had his misadventure in Padua, on *terra firma*, if he had fallen getting out his car, everyone would have condoled with him. Traffic lights are not funny, but it is funny to have one in Venice, over a canal-intersection. The same with the Venetian fire brigade. The things of *this* world reveal their essential absurdity when they are put in the Venetian context. In the unreal realm of the canals, as in a Swiftian Lilliput, the real world, with its contrivances, appears as a vast folly" *(Venice Observed* [Paris, 1956], p. 25).

[56]Concepts of the comic and the nature of a comedy are inextricably fused in Elizabethan criticism. The entries under "comedy" in Tudor and early Stuart dictionaries make it "an interlude, wherein the common vices of men and women are apparently declared in personages"; Cicero's "imitatio vitae, speculum consuetudinis & imago veritatis"; and "a base kind of poetry which endeth troublesome matters merrily." See the useful listing of such entries in Madeleine Doran's *Endeavors of Art* (Madison, Wis., 1954), pp. 382–384 (from which I quote). The complex and far-ranging roots of Renaissance comic theory have been ably studied by Marvin T. Herrick, *Comic Theory in the Sixteenth Century* (Urbana, Ill., 1964).

[57]In his *Dictionarium Linguae Latinae et Anglicanae* (Latin-English, 1588?) Thomas Thomas typically defines a comedy as "a play, wherein as in a glass, the image of civil and private living is represented, an interlude. It beginneth sorrowfully, and endeth merrily, contrary to a tragedy" (as quoted by Miss Doran from the fifth edition, revised, 1596).

[58]Sidney, *The Complete Works*, III, 39.

[59]Heywood, *An Apology for Actors* (1612), reprinted with an introduction and bibliographical notes by Richard H. Perkinson (New York, 1941), sigs. F3v–F4.

[60]Milton Crane has argued that "such a definition, in which echoes of other Elizabethan critics may be discerned, embraces every kind of comedy and obviates the need for Coghill's two categories," Shakespearean "romantic comedy" and Jonsonian "corrective comedy" *(Shakespeare Quarterly*, VI [1955], 3).

[61]The student of Elizabethan drama will immediately think of passages in it that parallel more or less the points made by Heywood; for example, *A Most Pleasant Comedie of Mucedorus* (1598):

> *Comedie* is mild, gentle, willing for to please,
> And seekes to gaine the loue of all estates.
> Delighting in mirth, mixt all with louely tales,
> And bringeth things with treble ioy to passe. (sig. A2^v)

The frequent appearance of "mirth" and "merry" in comment on comedy in Shakespeare's England shows it reflective of what is vital in my concept of the fundamentally comic—the spirit of free, irresponsible play; and perhaps it reminds our distracted age of how faded these words are nowadays. At least we still say "Merry Christmas!" whatever we may mean.

[62]John Dover Wilson, *The Fortunes of Falstaff* (Cambridge, 1944), p. 20, echoing, of course, Prospero.

CHAPTER II

[1]K. M. Lea, *Italian Popular Comedy* (Oxford, 1934), I, 184–185. Miss Lea's understanding of the farcical is consonant with my (independent) explication of the radically comic or the farcical. I move toward the romantic comedy that is Shakespeare's forte. For the moment I accept Miss Lea's differentiation of romantic comedy of intrigue and farce comedy. Attitude, as I have observed, is the surest thread through the mazes of the comic and its kin and the plays compounded of them.

[2]"The plot becomes a sort of mathematical exhibition of the maximum number of erroneous combinations of four people taken in pairs" (H. B. Charlton, *Shakespearian Comedy* [London, 1938], p. 66). E. K. Chambers finds the play illustrative of "farce . . . as the deduction of a logical conclusion from absurd premises. The playwright starts with some impossible assumption, which you must take for granted; however unconvincing, however grotesque, it is beyond criticism. From this he proceeds, without any further breach of the probabilities, to show what follows, and to work out a resulting tissue of absurdities, all inherent in the initial situation" *(Shakespeare: A Survey* [London, 1935], p. 28). Chambers thinks this basic assumption in *The Comedy of Errors* acceptable—but not the one that the Antipholus and Dromio of Syracuse, brought up by Ægeon until eighteen and out to seek their brothers, would show the obliviousness that they do; or that Ægeon would be so unperceptive as he is in the last scene. "One such assumption is . . . of the very essence of the game, but against a second we are entitled to protest. Had it not been for this lack of economy in the hypothesis, *The Comedy of Errors* would have presented the very pink and perfection of a farcical plot" (p. 30). But in the playhouse where in a true sense seeing is believing for the nonce an audience hardly halts in its fun to catch this flaw in the hypothesis of a rolling,

rollicking farce. What is more, we always know that truth is stranger than fiction—as any newspaper proves.

[3]G. L. Kittredge wrote a nicely appreciative paragraph on the variety and felicity of the meter of such verse (*The Complete Works of Shakespeare*, p. 134). I echo him.

[4]However, this view is countered by effective performances weaving in the interruptions and epilogue from *A Shrew* such as those seen at the Stratford-on-Avon Memorial Theater in 1953.

[5]After writing this sentence I found that Peter Alexander makes a strikingly similar reference to Burns's Tam in "The Original Ending of *The Taming of the Shrew*," in *Shakespeare Quarterly*, XX (Spring 1969), 115–116.

[6]Chambers, *Shakespeare: A Survey*, p. 27.

[7]Ibid., pp. 46–47.

[8]Ibid., pp. 47–48.

[9]Ibid., p. 170.

[10]Reasonably reliable tradition has it that Shakespeare's queen was so pleased with Falstaff in *1, 2 Henry IV* that she "commanded him to continue it for one Play more, and to shew him in Love" (Rowe in his *Life of Shakespeare* in 1709; cf. John Dennis in the epistle prefixed to *The Comicall Gallant* in 1702). See Kittredge, *The Complete Works of Shakespeare*, p. 63.

[11]Hazelton Spencer, *The Art and Life of William Shakespeare* (New York, 1940), p. 274.

CHAPTER III

[1]Santayana, *The Genteel Tradition at Bay*, in *Works*, Triton ed., VIII (New York, 1937), 139. Northrop Frye has given authoritative study under "Archetypal Criticism: Theory of Myths" to the literary forms that my book involves. For him, comedy illustrates "the mythos of spring"; romance, "the mythos of summer"; tragedy, "the mythos of autumn"; and satire, "the mythos of winter." See his *Anatomy of Criticism* (Princeton, N. J., 1957), pp. 158–239.

[2]Charlton, *Shakespearian Comedy*, p. 20. Detailed clarification of the term "romantic" as relevant to Shakespearean comedy emerges in the second chapter of this volume; to it I am much indebted.

[3]Ibid., pp. 79, 76, 74, 88, 92.

[4]Ibid., pp. 94–95.

[5]Ibid., p. 94.

[6]Chambers, *Shakespeare: A Survey*, p. 171.

[7]Charlton's pages on the play (*Shakespearian Comedy*, pp. 27–43) detail much that I point up.

[8]Ibid., p. 43.

[9]Ibid. Toward an inclusive definition of romance Henry James wrote: "The only *general* attribute of projected romance that I can see, the

only one that fits all its cases, is the fact of the kind of experience with which it deals—experience liberated, so to speak; experience disengaged, disembroiled, disencumbered, exempt from the conditions that we usually know to attach to it and, if we wish so to put the matter, drag upon it, and operating in a medium which relieves it, in a particular interest, of the inconvenience of a *related*, a measurable state, a state subject to all our vulgar communities. The greatest intensity may so be arrived at evidently—when the sacrifice of community, of the "related" sides of situations, has not been too rash. It must to this end not flagrantly betray itself; we must even be kept if possible, for our illusion, from suspecting any sacrifice at all. The balloon of experience is in fact of course tied to the earth, and under that necessity we swing, thanks to a rope of remarkable length, in the more or less commodious car of the imagination; but it is by the rope we know where we are, and from the moment that cable is cut we are at large and unrelated: we only swing apart from the globe—though remaining as exhilarated, naturally, as we like, especially when all goes well. The art of the romancer is, 'for the fun of it,' insidiously to cut the cable, to cut it without our detecting him" (Preface to *The American*, in *The Art of the Novel*, ed. R. P. Blackmur [New York, 1953], pp. 33–34). In *The Two Gentlemen* we abruptly detect the cutting of that "cable."

¹⁰Charlton. *Shakespearian Comedy*, p. 40.
¹¹Ibid., pp. 40–41.
¹²Ibid., p. 41.
¹³Kittredge, *Works*, p. 33.
¹⁴Charlton, *Shakespearian Comedy*, p. 42.
¹⁵Ibid.
¹⁶Ibid., pp. 42–43.

CHAPTER IV

¹I bypass such personal satire as many hold to be hidden in allusions to the contemporary scene. See the New Arden text, ed. Richard David (London, 1960), pp. xxxvii–1. My interest is limited to the timeless social satire directed at pretenses in conduct and manners that run counter to common sense.

²Kittredge, in *The Complete Works of Shakespeare*, p. 193. In trailing the movement of the play in this paragraph and the next I am indebted to G. P. Baker, *The Development of Shakespeare as a Dramatist* (New York, 1907), pp. 109–112.

³E. E. Stoll, *Shakespeare and Other Masters* (Cambridge, Mass., 1940), p. 13.

⁴The apt phrase is George Sherburn's (*A Literary History of England*,

p. 931). A more succinct definition of wit (as I would understand the term) could hardly be given.

⁵"Conventionally, high burlesque treats a trivial subject in an elevated manner, and low burlesque treats an elevated subject in a trivial manner. . . . Parody and mock-heroic belong to the family of high burlesque. Both use the grand manner for trifling themes, but parody adopts the manner of a specific work, while mock-heroic copies a whole class of writing. Conversely, travesty and the Hudibrastic poem are branches of low burlesque. Travesty imitates a particular model, the Hudibrastic a general type" (Worcester, *The Art of Satire*, pp. 47–48).

⁶Harley Granville-Barker, *Prefaces to Shakespeare* (Princeton, N. J., 1947), II, 426–427.

⁷Theodore Spencer, *Shakespeare and the Nature of Man* (Cambridge, Mass., 1943), p. 90.

⁸See above, note 5.

⁹Finding a tragic dimension in Shylock begins long before modern sensibility developed and the Nazis disgraced humanity. As early as 1709 Nicholas Rowe says that though he has seen Shylock enacted by a comic he cannot help thinking that he was intended tragically because of the intensity of his vindictiveness.

¹⁰See above, p. 15.

¹¹Entangled with this tragic aspect of Shylock is the alleged anti-Semitism of Shakespeare's portrait of the Jew. Kittredge declared: "One thing is clear, however: THE MERCHANT OF VENICE is no anti-Semitic document; Shakespeare was not attacking the Jewish people when he gave Shylock the villain's rôle. If so, he was attacking the Moors in *Titus Andronicus*, the Spaniards in *Much Ado*, the Italians in *Cymbeline*, the Viennese in *Measure for Measure*, the Danes in *Hamlet*, the Britons in *King Lear*, the Scots in *Macbeth*, and the English in *Richard the Third*" (*Works*, p. 258). Hazelton Spencer replied: "But his conception can not be whitewashed by comparing Shylock to Aaron, Iachimo, Angelo, Claudius, Edmund, Macbeth, Richard III, and Don John. True, all these are villains; but he also painted benevolent Moors, Italians, Viennese, Danes, Britons, Scots, and English. Though the Don was the national enemy, he even has one fairly admirable Spaniard. He never drew a noble Jew" (*The Art and Life of William Shakespeare*, p. 240). If one observes that Jessica is an admirable Jew, the reply is, I suppose, that she becomes so in Elizabethan eyes by turning Christian—not quite an accurate observation, and certainly one that Lorenzo would never have made. Perhaps the essential point is that Shakespeare's horizon was understandably limited by that of his day. For his times Jews were old foes of Christians and usurious money-lenders. He simply found among them a good villain for a romantic

comedy. As all students know, one has only to put Shylock beside Marlowe's Barabas to see the superior understanding with which Shakespeare portrays a villainous Jew. Barabas declines into a rankly melodramatic figure—even a farcical for some tastes.

[12]Bergson, finding the essence of the comic in the mechanization of the living, thinks repetition, inversion, and reciprocal interference of series are the techniques of the comic: "A continual change of aspect, the irreversibility of the order of phenomena, the perfect individuality of a perfectly self-contained series: such, then, are the outward characteristics—whether real or apparent is of little moment—which distinguish the living from the merely mechanical. Let us take the counterpart of each of these: we shall obtain three processes which might be called *repetition, inversion,* and *reciprocal interference of series.* Now, it is easy to see that these are also the methods of light comedy, and that no others are possible" *(Laughter,* p. 89).

[13]Nevill Coghill has remarked upon music as "Shakespeare's recurrent symbol of harmony"; see *The Merchant of Venice,* ed. J. R. Brown (Cambridge, Mass., 1959), p. li. W. H. Auden's "Music in Shakespeare" in *The Dyer's Hand and Other Essays* (London, 1962), pp. 500–527, is a general introduction to the dramatic functions of music and the use of instrumental music and songs in Shakespeare. Auden makes many perceptive observations in his "Notes on the Comic" in the same volume (pp. 371–385).

[14]To take the rhyming of the song ("bred"—"head") as a give-away of "lead" by Portia to Bassanio is, some would insist, to undercut the dramatic validity of the situation even though so doing would give it a certain farcical twist. See the survey of opinion on the moot point in *The Vocal Songs in the Plays of Shakespeare* (Cambridge, Mass., 1967, pp. 36–40) by Peter Seng; he sides with those who do hold that there is such a tip-off to Bassanio in the rhymes.

[15]Noted in R. G. Moulton, *Shakespeare as a Dramatic Artist,* Dover edition, with a new introduction by Eric Bentley (New York, 1966), p. 68.

[16]In this paragraph I am indebted to the introduction to the edition of the play by J. C. Smith in *Five Plays* (The Arden Shakespeare, ed. C. H. Herford [Boston, 1941]).

[17]Kittredge, editing *Much Ado* (Boston, 1941), p. 119.

[18]*The Sources of "Much Ado About Nothing": A Critical Study, Together with the Text of Peter Beverley's "Ariodanto and Ieneura"* (New Haven, 1950).

[19]"Similar hyperbole in the description of grief—and especially of weeping—occurs many times in Shakespeare, from his earliest plays to his latest. Usually it is in serious discourses, but now and then

the intent is humorous or satirical. In the present passage the extravagance of the idea is exquisitely appropriate to the half-serious, half-playful tone of the speaker" (Kittredge, editing *As You Like It* [Boston, 1939], p. 113).

[20]"The appearance of profound thought and careful logic in this sentence exemplifies a standard form of fool's humour. There is just enough sense in Touchstone's aphorism to make analysis possible. Sometimes, however, the jest consists in giving to punning or mere nonsense the air of logical reasoning or sententious wisdom" (Ibid., pp. 118–119). Such pure playfulness within the comic moment rides down quite any corrective intent in the comic spirit.

[21]Ibid., p. 127.

[22]Ibid., p. 126.

[23]Harley Granville-Barker commented astutely upon the values of the convention of the "boy as woman" in Elizabethan acting and its rich possibilities for comic effects (*A Companion to Shakespeare Studies*, ed. Harley Granville-Barker and G. B. Harrison [New York, 1940], pp. 54–56; and *Prefaces*, II, 434–435). See, too, Josephine Waters Bennett on the convention ("New Techniques of Comedy in *All's Well That Ends Well*," *Shakespeare Quarterly*, XVIII [1967], 344–345) and also Barber, pp. 243–247. The comic value of the convention of "boy as woman" in the drama is deepened when we remember that the Greek poet and politician Crites said that girls are charming only when they are a little boyish, and boys only when they are a little girlish (Werner Jaeger, *Paideia*, I [New York, 1945], 346). Effects comparable to Elizabethan ones hardly come when adult men, however skilful, take women's roles; witness, for example, the "in drag" production of *As You Like It* at the Old Vic in 1968. The impact of men in the roles cannot be that of Elizabethan boys, partly because we have had for centuries the tradition of women in women's roles. Nowadays adult men in them introduce a farcical note.

[24]Kittredge, editing *As You Like It*, p. 143.

[25]Jaques is, of course, using the word "humor" in its Elizabethan meaning of "bent," "inclination," or "disposition." Such a meaning has its background in medieval physiology that saw a preponderance of any one of the four "humors" in the body (bile, black bile, blood, and phlegm) as giving a man his particular nature or temperament —bilious, melancholic, sanguine, or phlegmatic.

[26]Kittredge, editing *As You Like It*, somewhat gravely assures us that Touchstone "is not really making light of the serious business of wedlock" in referring to the "small piece of work under way" as a "toy in hand." "He merely uses the courtly trick of depreciating one's self and one's own affairs" (p. 153). That no mockery is ultimately

intended appears when Touchstone bids Sir Oliver Martext farewell with a bit of the old ballad of "O swete Olyuer Leaue me not behind the[e]" and (perhaps) of the "Answer" to it (p. 154), and when the priest who has shown himself "scrupulous about the marriage ceremony" (p. 155) has the last word. Critical comedy in all the cruxes of human affairs allies itself with those extant conventions that time has tried and validated for coherent social life. It does not crusade for the ideal but finds in the actual what common sense can rest with.

[27]A super-ironic twist is given to this scene in that in actuality Rosalind and Orlando do wed by pledging their troth in the presence of a witness—as Celia is quickly aware.

[28]The reader will recall how I have limited my understanding of the shifting word "wit" to, essentially, "verbal markmanship." Of course over long time it has taken on many meanings; in the context just here "common sense," "natural wisdom," "intelligence," "mental agility," and "skill" might all be suggested.

[29]"Viola and Olivia and Duke Orsino have their prototypes in Riche, but are Shakespeare's own delightful creations. Sebastian is lightly sketched, but is quite worthy to be Viola's brother. No plausible suggestion has ever been made as a source for the underplot" (Kittredge, editing Twelfth Night [Boston, 1941], p. x).

[30]Ibid., p. 115.

[31]Ibid., p. 146.

[32]See, for example, the discussion in O. J. Campbell, Shakespeare's Satire (New York, 1943), pp. 84–88. I have held that the correctively comic can shade imperceptibly into the satiric (see above, pp. 20–21). And of course we should never forget that in a complexly interknit play any episode is modified in tone by its setting, its context in the whole—in this instance, a context permeated by humor that is at odds always with the genuinely satiric. Even the actor's style is relevant.

[33]It may be just worth noting that "notorious" is the very word that Malvolio uses to describe his "wrong" when he first appears in the concluding scene. Feste disguised as Sir Topas, and egged on by Sir Toby and Maria, treats sane Malvolio as a lunatic to be jeered at in an effort to deflate a conceited ass. Visiting a madhouse was fun for many of our forebears; and laughter at the absurdities of madness does underlie the amusement that the "all-licensed fool," often a man of addled wits who could speak sense within nonsense, gave in the Middle Ages. But a rational man does not normally laugh at genuine madness, at Lear and Ophelia. The Sweeper's comments in Dekker's 1 The Honest Whore (V.ii) show the comic approach to madness as amusing in Shakespeare's day; yet in the middle of the scene "Omnes" cry "A very piteous sight." Nowhere does Shakespeare laugh

at madness as such—a mark, surely, of his fine humanity.

[34]Kittredge, editing *Twelfth Night*, p. x.

[35]The Elizabethan stage fool or clown has a complex ancestry many times studied. Feste is no clumsy clown like his country cousin, the bumpkin who amuses us by the absurdities of his boorish manners or homely wit and wisdom that turn the tables on his social betters. He is far from the half-wit, entertaining by idiotic nonsense that yet makes a rough kind of sense. The mischief-making Vice of the old moralities and interludes is one of Feste's recognized ancestors that he himself acknowledges (IV.ii.134); but he is really a very smart fellow, a professional jester like Touchstone, "wise enough to play the fool," as Viola notes in classic lines on his art, and smart enough to extract gold coins for his pains. I borrow from the summary statement about the stage fool and his kindred in Kittredge's edition of *As You Like It* (pp. xiii–xv); but there are other good treatments of the subject. Classic books are Olive Mary Busby, *Studies in the Development of the Fool in Elizabehan Drama* (Oxford, 1923) and Enid Welsford, *The Fool: His Social and Literary History* (New York, n. d.); a notable recent one is Robert H. Goldsmith, *Wise Fools in Shakespeare* (East Lansing, Mich., 1955).

[36]See Chambers, as quoted above, pp. 166–167.

[37]"The Fiddler of Dooney," in W. B. Yeats, *The Collected Poems* (New York, 1956), p. 71. The phrase is quoted from John Unterecker, *A Reader's Guide to William Butler Yeats* (New York, 1959), p. 155.

[38]"New Techniques of Comedy in *All's Well That Ends Well*," *Shakespeare Quarterly*, XVIII (1967), 337–362; and *"Measure for Measure" as Royal Entertainment* (New York, 1966). Unlike my own, Mrs. Bennett's understanding of the nature of the comic is essentially that of Hobbes: we laugh out of a feeling of superiority to the object.

[39]Campbell, *Shakespeare's Satire*, pp. 98–120.

[40]*The Reader's Encyclopedia of Shakespeare*, ed. O. J. Campbell and Edward G. Quinn (New York, 1966), p. 896.

[41]Preface to *The Faithful Shepherdess*, ed. F. W. Moorman (London, 1897), p. 7. An arresting understanding of tragicomedy emerges in Cyrus Hoy's *Hyacinth Room: An Investigation into the Nature of Comedy, Tragedy, and Tragicomedy* (New York, 1964). Hoy "sees man as a dual figure, incongruously stretched between the ideal of his spiritual essence and the uncomfortable facts of his practical corporeal existence. The shifting relations of this basic incongruity, how it is viewed, whether accepted, rejected, or modified, promote the degrees of tragedy, comedy, and their intermediate state of tragicomedy" (*The Virginia Quarterly Review*, XLI [Winter 1965], xii).

[42]Frank Kermode, editing *The Tempest* (Cambridge, Mass., 1958), pp. liv–lv.

[43]E. M. W. Tillyard, *Shakespeare's Last Plays* (London, 1938).

[44]Kermode, editing *The Tempest*, p. lxxxi.

[45]Kittredge, editing *The Tempest* (Boston, 1939), p. xv.

[46]Ibid., p. 104.

[47]See above, p. 170.

[48]Kermode, editing *The Tempest*, p. 156.

[49]Ibid. (quoting Richmond Noble, *Shakespeare's Use of Song*, pp. 150–151).

[50]Kittredge, editing *The Tempest*, pp. 124–125.

[51]A most memorable association of music and sleep is met in another romance when Pericles hears "the music of the spheres" and cries: "Most heavenly music! / It nips me unto list'ning, and thick slumber / Hangs upon mine eyes. Let me rest" (*Pericles*, V.ii.234–236).

In lieu of trying to remark upon the modification of the comic by the masterly poetic in *The Tempest*, I refer my reader to Kermode, pp. lxxvii–lxxxi ("Verse—Imagery").

[52]But Kittredge, editing *The Tempest* (pp. xviii–xx), reminds us that "Shakespeare's Prospero, to the Elizabethan audience, was as comprehensible in his feats of magic as a chemist or an electrical engineer is to us moderns. His art is merely a method of controlling the forces of nature.... Prospero was no mere figure of impossible romance, tricked out with sorcerer's robe and book of spells to tickle their fancy for the marvellous. He belonged not only to a conceivable category among men, but to an established category. History and tradition knew such personages in the past—Friar Bacon and Bishop Grosseteste, and Albertus Magnus—who had mastered the secrets of nature beyond the limits of everyday experience. Eager students of the art abounded, and now and then one of them became eminent, as Prospero was eminent, for his control of the elements and his sovereignty over the human will." The play was "romance to the Elizabethans, but it was not the romance of unreality—its events were not beyond the possibilities of human life.... His agents are the elements, which he governs by the mysterious lore which has taught him to control the spirits of air and earth and fire and water. And these creatures are neither angels nor devils: they are but the elemental forces—conceived as personal—the serviceable *daemones* of theurgy (v, 1, 33–57)." We can, then, easily translate Prospero's magic into the marvels of science today—and deplore the failure of our "nobler reason" to use them fully for man's rational happiness on earth.

Chapter V

[1]Two notable readings are John Dover Wilson's in *The Fortunes of Falstaff* (New York, 1944) and C. L. Barber's in *Shakespeare's Festive*

Comedy (Princeton, N. J., 1959). For Wilson, Falstaff is essentially the Vice of the old moralities losing in his struggle to hold Prince Hal to a riotous way of life; for Barber, Falstaff is Carnival or a Lord of Misrule reigning in *1 Henry IV* and brought to trial in *2 Henry IV* for expulsion at the end of the play.

It is an interrogation *ad nauseam* for those who have heard the many discordant voices since Morgann spoke out resoundingly for the nays in *An Essay on the Dramatic Character of Sir John Falstaff* (1777). See my "Falstaff—Clown and Man," in *Studies in the English Renaissance Drama,* ed. Josephine Waters Bennett et al. (New York, 1959), pp. 345–356. This chapter is adapted from that essay.

³See above, pp. 12, 14, 16.

⁴Kittredge, editing *The First Part of King Henry IV* (Boston, 1940), p. xiii.

⁵A. C. Sprague ("Gadshill Revisited," *Shakespeare Quarterly,* IV [1953], 125–137) is surely conclusive on this matter even as E. E. Stoll has repeatedly been. For Stoll Falstaff in the playhouse is "apparently a coward and therefore one actually. The Falstaff of criticism, as the wisest critics have insisted or admitted, would not become apparent on the stage" *(From Shakespeare to Joyce* [New York, 1944], p. 197 n.). "Falstaff is plainly called a coward and (in various terms) a knave by those who ought to know, and in the action he as plainly so appears; and I do not see how in a theater, which, not a closet, is the only proper place of judgment, there could be any other opinion" (p. 225).

⁶*The First Part of King Henry IV,* pp. xii–xiv.

⁷E. E. Stoll, *Shakespeare and Other Masters* (Cambridge, Mass., 1940), p. 355. Cf. Stoll's *From Shakespeare to Joyce,* pp. 231–234.

⁸Kittredge "judges the character by the implications instead of (as the spectator should) by the positive impression" (Stoll, p. 233). Apologists for this comic device, this cowardly clown, misguidedly take him as a man in an actual world. They consider too curiously character at the expense of given situations manipulated for quickly amusing contrasts in the playhouse, where in a true sense seeing is believing for the nonce. These are the core concerns of any comic dramatist.

⁹Olive Mary Busby, *Studies in the Development of the Fool in Elizabethan Drama,* p. 56.

¹⁰Although he justly quotes *(From Shakespeare to Joyce,* p. 208) Dryden (and others) on Falstaff as "cowardly, drunken, amorous, vain, and lying" *(An Essay on Dramatic Poesy,* in *Essays of John Dryden,* ed. W. P. Ker [Oxford, 1926], I, 84, 215), Stoll does concede his "wit and merriment, his ingenuity, geniality, and infinite variety" *(From Shakespeare to Joyce,* p. 228).

¹¹Shakespeare's genius is too marked by sympathetic identification

with his creations to abide long with the radically comic; for sympathy is its mortal foe even as it is that of the satiric. His comic strain generally yields to humor and lyricism, even to music and dance, as we have seen. M. A. Shaaber has written to my point in observing how Shakespeare's "characteristic inability to hold to the detached position" vitiates to a degree the comic and satiric impact of *Troilus and Cressida* (*Shakespeare Quarterly,* IV [1953], 180). Sympathy (as with Goldsmith) is always breaking through. See above, pp. 21–23.

[12]Kittredge, *The Complete Works,* p. 582. "Falstaff, infatuated, has doomed himself."

[13]Cf. above, p. 15.

[14]Students who have held that Falstaff is no coward have usually protested his rejection even as those who have found him a stage coward have usually accepted it. Surely sentiment is dominant in the former folk. In holding Falstaff no coward, yet seeing the justice of his fate, Kittredge was exceptional. Although his astute awareness of the comic and quick appreciation of the world of the theater and its conventions seldom failed him, he was simply charmed, I think, into writing his arresting defense of Falstaff as no coward by the matchless wit, humor, and love of life in Falstaff the man to whom I am now attending. How otherwise account for the "denial of what in the theater seems obvious, the fact of cowardice" (Sprague, "Gadshill Revisited," p. 126) by a canny Boston Yankee and great scholar of Johnsonian common sense—the while the Doctor himself, as quoted by Malone, in reply to Morgann had declared that " 'all he shd. say, was, that if Falstaff was no coward, Shakespeare knew nothing of his art' " (*Boswell's Life of Johnson,* ed. G. B. Hill and L. F. Powell [Oxford, 1934], IV, 515)?

[15]*The Life of King Henry the Fifth,* ed. G. L. Kittredge (Boston, 1945), p. 133.

[16]Cf. above, p. 15.

[17]Leslie Hotson, "Falstaff's Death and Greenfield's," *The Times Literary Supplement,* April 6, 1956, p. 212.

[18]But we blur the lines of the clown in his amoral moments unless our recognition of them extends quickly to the moral frame of reference that surrounds them: "To examine the question of his cowardice as if he were a man like other men is to miss the point of his role.... Cowardice can only exist when standards of honour exist to be violated: and Falstaff is the ape of honour, whose views on the subject are known. This does not mean that he is open to moral condemnation.... He does not belong in the realm of moral judgements" (M. C. Bradbrook, *Shakespeare and Elizabethan Poetry* [London, 1951], pp. 198–199). Miss Bradbrook comprehends one dimension of Falstaff, his stature in the amoral moment as a clown-tool of the radically comic; and she

recognizes that "cowardice can only exist when standards of honour exist to be violated." But she misses, I think, Falstaff's stature as a man-clown in failing to see that he eventually is "open to moral condemnation" if only by his irresponsible way with those "standards of honour" over time—in the world of Hal become Henry V.

[19]If fat folk usually have more humor than lean, it may be because they usually have more buoyant animal health; good health underlies the freely comic; "no melancholy man was ever fat, as King James rightly argued" (Lily Bess Campbell, *Shakespeare's Tragic Heroes: Slaves of Passion* [New York, reprinted 1952], p. 113).

[20]Robert Langbaum has shown how psychological criticism since Morgann's day has constantly distended character in drama at the expense of action involving accepted moral standards and, hence, inevitably moved the genre toward the dramatic monologue. Langbaum would point the way toward peace between traditional dramatic criticism and modern psychological criticism: "For if we conceive the play as larger than the plot, the part of character uncovered by psychological criticism falls not outside the play but outside the moral categories of the plot. The plot, which we understand through moral judgment, becomes a clearing in the forest; while the play shades off to include the penumbra of forest fringe out of which the plot has emerged, a penumbra which we apprehend through sympathy. Such a conception makes room for psychological criticism by dissolving the limits of character and of the play, by suggesting that the limits are always in advance of comprehension. That is how we come by the modern idea of a masterpiece as an enigma whose whole meaning can never be formulated. Comprehension becomes an unending process, historical and evolutionary; while the play itself moves inviolate down the ages, eluding final formulation yet growing, too, in beauty and complexity as it absorbs into its meaning everything that has been thought and felt about it" ("Character Versus Action in Shakespeare," *Shakespeare Quarterly*, VII [1957], 64–65). Within Langbaum's woodland the Stoll lion and the Morgann lamb are to lie down together and Falstaff be indisputably, and unendingly, more than a mere clown. But surely the Globe Falstaff cavorted in the clearing in that forest, not in the penumbra of its fringe. The deep forest is, I suppose, the habitat of Beckett's clowns in *Waiting for Godot*.

CHAPTER VI

[1]See above, pp. 9–11.

[2]See J. V. Cunningham, *Woe and Wonder: The Emotional Effect of Shakespearean Tragedy* (Denver, Colo., 1951).

[3]Alexander Pope, *An Essay on Man*, Epistle II, 11. 13–18, in *The*

Complete Poetical Works, Student's Cambridge ed. (Boston, 1903), p. 142.

[4]My short shrift with large matters that have stretched critical wits for ages may seem comical to experts. I would merely recognize tragic elements that throw into relief the nature of the comic as I conceive it. Various understandings of *catharsis* and *hamartia* need not arrest us. Peter Alexander ably handles both terms in *Hamlet: Father and Son* (Oxford, 1955). Santayana would find the essence of tragedy in "the sense of the finished life, of the will fulfilled and enlightened: that purging of the mind so much debated upon, which relieves us of pent-up energies, transfers our feelings to a greater object, and thus justifies and entertains our dumb passions, detaching them at the same time for a moment from the accidental occasions of our earthly life" (*Interpretations of Poetry and Religion* [New York, 1927], p. 281).

[5]Even two of its peripheral characters have recently inspired a popular play (Tom Stoppard's *Rosencrantz and Guildenstern Are Dead*) that focuses something of the tragic predicament of the common man in our time.

[6]"Horatio is a sedate person, constitutionally disposed to mild pleasantries. Cf. i, 5, 125, 126; iii, 2, 93, 94, 290, 296; iv, 6, 7; v, 2, 162, 163" (Kittredge, editing *Hamlet* [Boston, 1939], p. 131).

[7]Quoted in *Hamlet*, Furness Variorum Edition (1877), I, 136.

[8]My "Polonius in the Round," *Shakespeare Quarterly*, IX (1958), 83–85, is a fuller facing of such a reading.

[9]For Lily B. Campbell, Polonius is little more than "the faithful ears and prompt reporter of a tyrant," of a murderer and usurper ("Polonius: The Tyrant's Ears," *Joseph Quincy Adams: Memorial Studies*, pp. 295–313). She and others deny Polonius enough dignity to give him any tragic stature and to preserve his comic and ironic impact that must hinge on presented contrasts between actualities and appearances.

[10]O. J. Campbell, *Shakespeare's Satire*, pp. 150, 159. Some have wrongly held that Hamlet's assumed "madness" becomes more than skin deep when at moments he is distraught and nearly hysterical. In his speech to Laertes (V.ii.237–255) just before the fatal duel Hamlet's equivocation about his "madness" as leading to his wronging of Laertes—as being really "poor Hamlet's enemy"—must be accepted as but a sustaining of the deceit that the "antic disposition" initally "put on" necessitated. See Kittredge, editing *Hamlet*, pp. 293–294.

[11]I have been observing how Hamlet as a "mad" fool speaks out with barbed wit and satiric bite. The subtly comic and ironic aspects of Hamlet playing that role after he has "put an antic disposition on" have been disclosed by Harry Levin (*The Question of Hamlet* [New York, 1959]). He recalls Gilbert Murray's noting that Shakespeare not only did wonders with the real fool but in a sense made his greatest

tragic hero out of the fool transfigured. He thinks Murray might well have gone on to note that Hamlet re-enacts "the classical *eiron,* the Socratic ironist who practices wisdom by disclaiming it." Hamlet "stoops to folly in the grand Erasmian manner" because he knows that life is a comedy in which each man plays his part in one disguise or another. If not like Lear companioned by a fool, Hamlet yet has his fool in the dead Yorick, fittingly in view of the play's concern with death. "Since Yorick is a *muta persona,* whose gibes and gambols and songs are conspicuous by their silence, they are anticipated by the riddles and gags and equivocations of the Clown as First Grave-digger. The Prince plays straight man to him. . . . What follows, when the clown identifies Yorick, is the gloomiest of recognition-scenes. The fool's traditional function has been to demonstrate that the other person, whatever his pretensions to wit may be, is likewise a fool; their dialectic, be it erratic or subtle, inevitably terminates with *tu quoque.* Here, however, the poles of the argument are no longer wisdom and folly but life and death" (Levin, pp. 122–125). I turn to the gravediggers' scene for its playhouse impact in terms of my understanding of the comic.

¹²Santayana, *Soliloquies,* p. 6.

¹³"The language and manners of Osric are a good-natured satire on the affectations of many young gentlemen at the English court. One of the peculiarities of his style is the use of words in a forced or unusual sense. Polonius has a touch of the same affectation" (Kittredge, editing *Hamlet,* p. 287).

¹⁴Jean S. Calhoun, "*Hamlet* and the Circumference of Action," *Renaissance News,* XV (1962), 282–283.

¹⁵In telling of an amusing incident in the drawing room of Lady Ottoline Morrell, Santayana gives a civilized perspective on obscenity, one largely lost today. Calling and finding the lady out, he was left alone to await her. "I picked up a beautifully bound small book that lay at hand on the table. It was a French tale of the eighteenth century, and as obscene as possible. Naturally I read on in it, for I like obscenity well enough in its place, which is behind the scenes, or bursting out on occasion in a comic, rollicking, enormously hearty mood, as in Aristophanes; and when Lady Ottoline arrived, and found me reading it, she took pains to say it was not her book, but Mr. Strachey's. Certainly it wasn't likely to be her book; but he might have put it in his pocket, and not left it lying on the drawing-room table" (*My Host the World* [New York, 1953], pp. 94–95).

¹⁶See, for example, Robert A. Watts, "The Comic Scenes in *Othello,*" in *Shakespeare Quarterly,* XIX (1968), 349–354.

¹⁷Bernard Spivack holds that Shakespeare's "vivacious villains" like Iago and Richard III "exist in tragedy and are, in fact, a form of comic

variation within the serious movement of the tragic theme." Their
biting, sardonic wit gives us subtle perspective on an absurd aspect
of the protagonists. "In comedy, which needs a variation in reverse,
his villains have solemn, even somber, natures. The distinction is
moral as well as dramatic: when the good world is serious, its villainy
is jovial; and the same proposition reverses itself in comedy" *(Shakespeare and the Allegory of Evil* [New York, 1958], p. 408). In the first
and last mature romantic comedies that I reviewed there is no true
villain; Puck is just the "pert and nimble spirit of mirth" in action,
and Malvolio is little more than the foe of cakes and ale.

[18]My "Shakespeare's Enobarbus," in *Joseph Quincy Adams: Memorial
Studies,* pp. 391–408, is a detailed study of the character.

[19]See Ionesco, quoted above, p. 16.

[20]Comic episodes and characters in the tragedies proper fall roughly
into two groups—organic and inorganic ones. Such characters as Mercutio, Polonius, and Lear's Fool are vitally necessary "to give circumstance to the plot or to prepare for some climax that is coming after
them." The others—such as the porter in *Macbeth,* the peasant who
brings Cleopatra the asps, and the clown in *Othello*—touch for only
a single moment "the outermost fringe of the story, and then . . .
[disappear] entirely from the stage." Such a character "understands no
whit of the tragedy which is gathering round him"; he does not
dream that he is "witnessing the crisis of a tragedy or that he has
any part in bringing it about. Yet his experience is that of every one
of us in that we constantly touch tragic activities without any awareness
of their import" (William Hadow, "The Use of the Comic Episodes
in Tragedy," in *Collected Essays* [London, 1928], pp. 327–330). Such
characters add immeasurably to our sense of the sweep of the tragic
world in Shakespeare, to its truth. Willard Farnham stresses the "theme
of unsimple truth," abundantly present in *Hamlet,* and "so subtly
extended that it is everywhere in the action and the poetry" and so
complex that it includes "even a composition of low comedy with
high seriousness" (editing *Hamlet* [Baltimore, 1957], pp. 22, 19).

[21]"Wanton and transitory as our existence is, and comic as it must
appear in the eyes of the happy gods, it is all in all to our mortal
nature; and whilst intellectually we may judge ourselves somewhat
as the gods might judge us, and may commend our lives to the keeping
of eternity, our poor animal souls are caught inextricably in the toils
of time, which devours us and all our possessions. The artist playing
a farce for others suffers a tragedy in himself. When he aspires to
shed as much as possible the delusions of earthly passion and to look
at things joyfully and unselfishly, with the clear eyes of youth, it is
not because he feels no weight of affliction, but precisely because

he feels its weight to the full, and how final it is" (Santayana, *Soliloquies in England,* p. 6).

²²"We are dealing with a play, something to be bodied forth on the stage before an audience, not a dramatic poem designed for the unrestrained compass of the individual reader's imagination" (John Lawlor, *The Tragic Sense in Shakespeare* [London, 1960], p. 108).

²³Hamlet's beloved father has been foully murdered by his brother who has whored Hamlet's mother. One may wonder what additional "objective correlative" (in his famous phrase) T. S. Eliot could have suggested as adequate for evoking and focusing Hamlet's emotions.

CHAPTER VII

¹Worcester, *The Art of Satire,* pp. 140–141. My debt to Worcester's book is great, as quotations in this chapter and the first suggest.

²Ibid., p. 142.

³Ibid., p. 129.

⁴Ibid., p. 107.

⁵Ibid., p. 166. Irony "is abused when it is treated as a canal through which the stream of life is diverted into ridicule and absurdity. It is an intellectual instrument, and it demands a creative purpose. The high seriousness that burns through Swift's elaborate trifling, his moral integrity and quintessential sanity, and the amazing purposefulness of every one of his ironical compositions are the pillars on which his greatness rests. Irony is negative in its nature. It reaches the height of its electric force only when it is used for a positive, creative purpose. Lacking such purpose, romantic irony and cosmic irony at their most extravagant convey an impression of megalomania and frustration—of weakness, not of strength" (Worcester, *The Art of Satire,* pp. 143–144).

⁶Ibid., p. 136.

⁷Ibid., p. 168.

⁸"All is a tale told, if not by an idiot, at least by a dreamer; but it is far from signifying nothing" (Santayana, "A Brief History of My Opinions," in *The Philosophy of Santayana,* ed. Irwin Edman [New York, 1936], p. 19). Compare: "Perhaps the universe is nothing but an equilibrium of idiocies" (Santayana, *Persons and Places* [New York, 1944], p. 127). The author of *The Life of Reason* would surely have stressed "equilibrium" in this sentence and left its last word to the "absurdists" in modern drama.

⁹At least four distinguished scholar-critics have justly condemned Kott's influential *Shakespeare Our Contemporary* (Garden City, N. Y., 1964): "The worst essays are on *The Tempest* and *A Midsummer Night's Dream.* . . . Here is the misrepresentation of all earlier criticism to make

one's own version seem more strikingly original.... The *Lear* piece has many of the defects of the others—rhetorical extravagance, muddled method, failure to profit by other insights, a weakness for striking but improbable historical parallels and inferences. Yet it is much the best of all the essays" (Frank Kermode, "The Shakespearean Rag," in *The New York Review of Books*, Vol. III, No. 3 [September 24, 1964], p. 10). Kott "sees a preview of Sputnik in Puck's earth-girdling and a glimpse of James Dean in Hamlet's disquietude.... But the basic issue lies between an approach which is vaguely existentialist and a world view which was profoundly humanistic" (Harry Levin, *Yale Review*, LIV [1964], 261, 263). See, too, Alfred Harbage's devastating way with Kott in "Shakespeare East and West," in *Harvard Today* (May, 1972), p. 4. Surely "there is greater enrichment in the effort to know Shakespeare fully than in the effort to diminish him to the stature of Our Contemporary" (A. S. Downer, *Book Week*, October 4, 1964, p. 31).

[10]*The Collected Poems of W. B. Yeats* (New York, 1956), p. 139.

[11]Santayana, *Soliloquies*, p. 141. The full passage is relevant: "We are caught in the meshes of time and place and care; and as the things we have set our heart on, whatever they may be, must pass away in the end, either suddenly or by a gentle transformation, we cannot take a long view without finding life sad, and all things tragic.... It is a true aspect of existence in one relation and on a certain view; but to take this long view of existence, and look down the avenues of time from the station and with the emotions of some particular moment, is by no means inevitable, nor is it a fair and sympathetic way of viewing existence. Things when they are actual do not lie in that sort of sentimental perspective, but each is centred in itself; and in this intrinsic aspect existence is nothing tragic or sad, but rather something joyful, hearty, and merry. A buoyant and full-blooded soul has quick senses and miscellaneous sympathies: it changes with the changing world; and when not too much starved or thwarted by circumstances, it finds all things vivid and comic. Life is free play fundamentally and would like to be free play altogether. In youth anything is pleasant to see or to do, so long as it is spontaneous, and if the conjunction of these things is ridiculous, so much the better: to be ridiculous is part of the fun" (pp. 140–141). Many souls nowadays are so "starved or thwarted by circumstances" (or their own irrational desires) that whatever comic view they achieve is that of "black" comedy. Yet some Negro men and women, however, "starved or thwarted by circumstances" and full of righteous sorrow and anger, rise above such feelings, find "all things vivid and comic," and write plays rich in humor, wit, and genuine humanity; for example, Douglas Turner

Ward's *Day of Absence*, Lorraine Hansberry's *To Be Young, Gifted, and Black*, and Micki Grant's *Don't Bother Me—I Can't Cope*.

[12]Santayana, *Soliloquies*, p. 132.

[13]Ibid., pp. 102–103. "Now laughter, as I have come to see in my old age, is the innocent youthful side of repentance, of disillusion, of understanding. It liberates incidentally, as spiritual insight liberates radically and morally" (Santayana, *The Middle Span* [New York, 1945], p. 109).

[14]Santayana, *My Host the World*, pp. 101–102.

[15]See Martin Esslin, *The Theatre of the Absurd* (Garden City, N. Y., 1961); Robert Brustein, *The Theatre of Revolt* (London, 1965); and George E. Wellwarth, *The Theater of Protest and Paradox* (New York, 1967). Brustein finds the "theatre of revolt" ultimately in revolt against life itself.

[16]Santayana, *The Life of Reason*, p. 411.

[17]"Absurd" is a pivotal word for existentialists. Santayana recognizes with Sartre and Camus the fundamental absurdity of existence. But he writes: "The dismay that has fallen of late upon so many minds has not touched me. I have never had any illusions about the world's being rationally guided or true to any ideals; reason and ideals arise in doing well something that at bottom there was no reason for doing." Yet his dominant interest is the art of rational life for the individual in an irrational world as the Greeks first defined that art; and he adds that "it is possible to live nobly in this world only if we live in another world ideally" (*Twentieth Century Authors*, ed. Stanley J. Kunitz and Howard Haycraft [New York, 1942], p. 1231).

Esslin's *The Theatre of the Absurd* concludes (p. 316) with significant sentences. The next to the last reads: "For the dignity of man lies in his ability to face reality in all its senselessness; to accept it freely, without fear, without illusions—and to laugh at it." Santayana would have agreed, I think. Esslin's last sentence runs: "That is the cause to which, in their various individual, modest, and quixotic ways, the dramatists of the Absurd are dedicated." But—however understandably—theirs is not the free and happy laughter described by Santayana and illustrated by Shakespeare.

[18]In *The Life of Reason* (first edition in 1905–1906, second edition with a new preface in 1924, and revised edition in 1954) Santayana defined the nature of reason in what might be called the "first principles" of thought, in society, in religion, in art, and in science. The "Life of Reason . . . is simply the unity given to all existence by a mind *in love with the good*. In the higher reaches of human nature, as much as in the lower, rationality depends on distinguishing the excellent; and that distinction can be made, in the last analysis, only

by an irrational impulse. As life is a better form given to force, by which the universal flux is subdued to create and serve a somewhat permanent interest, so reason is a better form given to interest itself, by which it is fortified and propagated, and ultimately, perhaps, assured of satisfaction. The substance to which this form is given remains irrational; so that rationality, like all excellence, is something secondary and relative, requiring a natural being to possess or to impute it. When definite interests are recognised and the values of things are estimated by that standard, action at the same time veering in harmony with that estimation, then reason has been born and a moral world has arisen" (*The Life of Reason*, pp. 7–8). Reason so understood by a poetic naturalist is as far from Blake's "mind-forg'd manacles" as from Lawrence's "blood knowledge." It is a harmony of thinking and feeling. If opposed to mysticism and anti-intellectualism, it is capacious enough to embrace insight and inspiration. Intelligence that fructifies in such reason is "the highest form of vitality" for Santayana.

[19]Virginia Woolf observed: "One advantage of having a settled code of morals is that you know exactly what to laugh at" (quoted by Katherine Anne Porter in reviewing E. M. Forster's *Two Cheers for Democracy* in *The New York Times Book Review*, November 4, 1951, p. 3). Today when moral codes are in flux, many men laugh indiscriminately at anything and everything.

[20]Santayana, *Interpretations of Poetry and Religion* (New York, 1927), p. 261. Such words are at once a bow and a rebuke to men who exalt the irrational.

[21]Santayana, *The Middle Span*, p. 40.

[22]Theodore Spencer, *Shakespeare and the Nature of Man*, p. ix.

[23]Any reader will think of many current productions in which the directors and producers do as they please with the texts to reduce Shakespeare to "our contemporary."

[24]Santayana, *Character and Opinion in the United States* (New York, 1924), pp. vii–viii.

[25]Santayana, *The Life of Reason*, p. 82.

[26]Santayana, *The Realm of Matter* (New York, 1930), p. vii.

[27]*The Life of Reason*, p. 375.

[28]*Soliloquies*, p. 97.

[29]Ibid., p. 6.

[30]Edmund Wilson has written of Santayana: "the intelligence that has persisted in him has been that of the civilized human race" (*Europe Without Baedeker* [Garden City, N. Y., 1966], pp. 54–55). For Wallace Stevens, Santayana dying in Rome was "master and commiserable man, . . . The one invulnerable man among / Crude captains" ("To an Old Philosopher in Rome," in *The Collected Poems* [New York, 1967].

pp. 509–510). In his later years Santayana increasingly commended and illustrated a life of detached withdrawal and contemplation, of communion with essence—to use the word to which he gave a new dimension. Such absorption in the spiritual life as he understood it has drawn hostile comment from folk justly concerned for this world's work. But Santayana never disavowed his primary commitment to the life of reason for the world of affairs. His late devotion to the life contemplative might generously be seen as an ultimate manifestation of reason and wisdom in an aged man, acutely aware of the tragic lack of reason in the modern world, and of his impending entrance into eternity.

If my presentation of Santayana has focused upon his naturalism and his definition of the life of reason rather than upon his "Platonism," it is because his understanding of the comic rests upon his awareness of the "realm of matter." I would not minimize his awareness of the "realm of essence," the "realm of truth," and the "realm of spirit."

[31]Santayana, *Reason in Common Sense* (New York, 1924), p. 252 (omitted from the revised edition of *The Life of Reason* in 1954).

[32]*Soliloquies*, p. 94.

[33]*The Life of Reason*, p. 287.

[34]Ibid., p. 283.

[35]Santayana, *The Realm of Essence* (New York, 1927), p. xix. This quotation ends an essay on Santayana by Horace M. Kallen ("The Laughing Philosopher," in *The Journal of Philosophy*, LXI [1964], 19–35), unknown to me until I had finished this study. The essay admirably reveals the laughter beyond the tears of things that is heard in the late Santayana.

[36]W. H. Auden, "September 1, 1939," in *The Collected Poetry* (New York, 1945), p. 59.

INDEX

Adams, Joseph Quincy, 162, 178, 180
Aeschylus, 1
Alexander, Peter, 167, 178
All's Well That Ends Well, 113, 171, 173
Amphitruo, 37
Antony and Cleopatra, 134, 144–45
Apology for Actors, An, 165
Apolonius and Silla, 101
Arcadia, 47
Ariosto, Lodovico, 39, 48, 79
Aristophanes, 1, 4, 14, 20, 54, 160, 179
Aristotle, 2, 4, 30
Arnold Matthew, 64
Arte of Rhetorique, The, 159
As You Like It, 77, 89–101, 102, 112, 171, 173
Auden, W. H., 160–61, 170, 185

Bacon, Friar, 174
Baker, G. P., 168
Bandello, Matteo, 79, 101
Barber, C. L., 161, 171, 175
Baugh, Albert C., 163
Beckett, Samuel, 30, 147, 177

Belleforest, François de, 79
Bennett, Josephine Waters, 113, 171, 173, 175
Bentley, Eric, 162, 170
Bergson, Henri, 2, 3, 158, 170
Beverley, Peter, 170
Blackmur, R. P., 168
Blake, William, 184
Boswell, James, 176
Bradbrook, M. C., 176–77
Brecht, Bertolt, 16, 19, 162
Brereton, Cloudesley, 158
Brill, A. A., 164
Brown, J. R., 170
Brueghel, Peter, 163
Brustein, Robert, 183
Bullough, Geoffrey, 160
burlesque, nature of, 23–24, 71, 161, 169
Burns, Robert, 167
Busby, Olive Mary, 173, 175
Byron, Lord, 9

Calhoun, Jean S., 141, 179
Campbell, Lily Bess, 177, 178
Campbell, O. J., 114, 138, 172, 173, 178
Camus, Albert, 183

Cazamian, Louis, 161, 163
Cervantes, Miguel de, 15
Chairs, The, 16
Chambers, E. K., 40–41, 43, 49–50, 166, 167, 173
Chaplin, Charlie, 19, 161
Charles II, King, 4
Charlton, H. B., 48, 53–54, 166, 167, 168
Chaucer, Geoffrey, 4, 43, 47, 54, 64, 67, 95, 149, 161
Chekov, Anton, 161
Cicero, 2, 165
clown, nature of the, 6–9, 53–54, 60. *See also* fool
Coghill, Nevill, 165, 170
Coleridge, Samuel Taylor, 146
Collier, Jeremy, 3
Comedy of Errors, The, 36–39, 47–48, 55, 57, 72, 74, 102, 110
comic, nature of the, 2–4 (classical concepts), 5–23, 31 (comedy defined), 32–33 (Elizabethan definition of a comedy), 33–35, 37–38, 54–55, 93, 125–26, 127–29, 136, 139–40, 145, 151 ("black" comedy), 158 (Bergson), 160, 162, 163–64 (Freud), 164–65, 165 (Elizabethan definition of comedy), 170 (Bergson), 182 ("black" comedy)
Comicall Gallant, The, 167
Condell, Henry, 1
Congreve, William, 3
contrast, comic use of, 31, 53–54, 109, 164–65
Cooper, Lane, 158
Cory, Daniel, 162
Crane, Milton, 165
Cunningham, J. V., 177
Cymbeline, 114, 124, 169

dance, relation to the comic of the, 86–87, 104, 112, 123
Daumier, Honoré, 163
David, Richard, 168
Day of Absence, 182

Dean, James, 182
Dekker, Thomas, 172
Democritus, 18
Dennis, John, 167
De Quincey, Thomas, 143–44
de Sola Pinto, Vivian, 159
Despois, Eugène, 158
Diana, 50–51, 68
Dickens, Charles, 4, 14–15, 104, 160
Dictionarium Linguae Latinae et Anglicanae, 165
disguise and mistaken identity, relation to the comic of, 37, 59, 77, 96–97, 101–103. *See also* transvestism
"dogberryisms," nature of, 83–84
Don't Bother Me—I Can't Cope, 182
Doran, Madeleine, 165
Downer, A. S., 182
drama, definition of the, 30–31, 52
drunkenness, comic use of, 39, 103, 119, 129, 143–44
Dryden, John, 2, 3, 64, 175

Einstein, Albert, 154
Edman, Irwin, 181
Elizabeth I, Queen, 44
Eliot, T. S., 181
Empson, William, 26
Erasmus, Desiderius, 17
Esslin, Martin, 162, 183
Euphues, 59
Every Man in his Humour, 158
Every Man out of his Humour, 158

farce, nature of, 16 (nearness to tragic), 35–38, 40–41, 43–44, 166
Farnham, Willard, 162, 180
Feuillerat, Albert, 164
Fielding, Henry, 61
Fletcher, John, 115
fool, nature of the, 109, 111, 145,

172–73, 178–79. *See also* clown
Forster, E. M., 184
Francis, Saint, 17
Freud, Sigmund, 24, 28, 154, 163–64
Frye, Northrop, 161, 167
Fujimura, Thomas H., 159

Gammer Gurton's Needle, 37
Gascoigne, George, 39
Gilbert, Sir William S., 52
Goldsmith, Oliver, 20, 21, 163, 176
Goldsmith, Robert H., 173
Goya, Francisco de, 163
Grant, Micki, 183
Granville-Barker, Harley, 66–67, 169, 171
Greville, Fulke, first Lord Brooke, 11
Grosseteste, Robert, 174

Hadow, William, 180
Hals, Frans, 163
Hamlet, 118, 119, 133–42, 145–46, 169, 178–79, 180
Hansberry, Lorraine, 183
Harbage, Alfred, 182
Harrison, G. B., 171
Hathaway, Ann, 43
Haycraft, Howard, 183
Heminges, John, 1
1, 2 Henry IV, 125–132, 167, 175
Henry V, 176
Herford, C. H., 158, 170
Heywood, Thomas, 32–33, 50, 165–66
Highet, Gilbert, 163
Hill, G. B., 176
Hitler, Adolf, 19
Hobbes, Thomas, 2, 4, 173
Hogarth, William, 163
Holzknecht, Karl J., 159
1 Honest Whore, The, 172
Hopkins, Gerard, 160
Horace, 21, 149
Hotson, Leslie, 131, 176

Housman, A. E., 9–10
Hoy, Cyrus, 173
humor, nature of, 14, 15–20, 22, 73, 82–83, 108–109, 133
Hutchinson, Thomas, 162
Huxley, Elsbeth, 163

Ibsen, Henrik, 43
imagery, nature of, 29–30
invective, nature of, 23
Ionesco, Eugène, 16, 20, 147, 180
irony, nature of, 23–24 (dramatic irony), 29, 58, 147–49 (cosmic irony), 181 (cosmic irony)
I Suppositi, 39

James, Henry, 167–68
James I, King, 177
Johnson, Samuel, 135, 138, 176
jokes, nature of, 64–65
Jonson, Ben, 2, 3, 4, 20, 22, 23, 32, 33, 114, 158
Joyce, James, 26, 175
Juvenal, 3, 21

Kallen, Horace M., 185
Keats, John, 9–10, 164
Ker, W. P., 175
Kermode, Frank, 117, 173, 174, 182
King Lear, 134, 145, 150, 169, 181
Kittredge, G. L., 53, 83, 94, 117, 126–27, 129, 162, 167, 168, 169, 170, 171, 172, 173, 174, 175, 176, 178, 179
Knight's Tale, The, 47, 67
Kott, Jan, 16, 150, 181–82
Kunitz, Stanley J., 183

Lamb, Charles, 19, 26, 27, 128, 162, 164
Lamb, Mary, 162
Langbaum, Robert, 177
laughter, the relation to the comic of, 2, 4–6, 159, 182, 183, 185
Lawlor, John, 181
Lawrence, D. H., 6, 184

Lea, K. M., 36, 166
L'Enfant Prodigue, 159
Levin, Harry, 178–79, 182
Lincoln, Abraham, 18
Lodge, Thomas, 89
love, comic use of, 68–69
Love's Labour's Lost, 55, 56–67, 72–73, 88
Lucian, 149
Lucretius, 160
Lyly, John, 53, 59–60, 61
lyrical, nature of the, 77–78, 160

Macbeth, 34, 143–44, 150, 169, 180
McCarthy, Mary, 165
Magnus, Albertus, 174
Malcontent, The, 139
Malone, Edmund, 176
Marceau, Marcel, 161
Marlowe, Christopher, 169
Marston, John, 114, 139
Marx, Karl, 154
masks, the relation to the comic of, 34
Massinger, Philip, 22
Measure for Measure, 113, 162, 169, 173
Menaechmi, 37
Merchant of Venice, The, 55, 74–79, 89, 169, 170
Meredith, George, 2, 3
Merry Wives of Windsor, The, 36, 43–45, 49–50, 55
Mesnard, Paul, 158
metaphor, the relation to the comic of, 27–29
Middleton, Thomas, 22
Midsummer Night's Dream, A, 64, 66, 67–74, 78, 79, 87, 116, 118
Miller, Jonathan, 162–63
mock-heroic, nature of the, 71, 169
Molière, Jean Baptiste, 1, 3, 20
Montemayor, Jorge de, 50–51
Moorman, F. W., 173
More, Life of Syr Thomas, 162

More, Sir Thomas, 17–18, 162
Morgan, Charles, 58
Morgann, Maurice, 125, 175, 177
Morrell, Lady Ottoline, 179
Moulton, R. G., 170
Mozart, Wolfgang Amadeus, 163
Mucedorus, A Most Pleasant Comedie of, 165–66
Much Ado About Nothing, 79–89, 112, 169, 170
Muir, Kenneth, 164
Murray, Gilbert, 178
music and song, the place in romantic comedy of, 11–12, 23, 67, 77–78, 112, 118, 121–22

names, comic use of, 61
New Way to Pay Old Debts, A, 22
Noble, Richmond, 174
Novelle (Bandello's), 101

Oakeshott, Michael, 159
obscene or bawdy material, comic use of, 54–55, 143–44
O'Hanlon, Redmond L., 164
O'Neill, Eugene, 31
Orwell, George, 155
Othello, 134, 143, 150, 179, 180
Ovid, 68

parody, nature of, 161, 169
pathetic, relation to the comic of the, 130–31
Pericles, 114, 116, 124, 174
Perkinson, Richard H., 165
Persius, 3
Plato, 2, 4, 141
Plautus, 37
Playboy of the Western World, The, 162
play, relation to the comic of, 6–7, 16, 150, 159
plot, definition of, 30
Plutarch, 67
Pope, Alexander, 177
Porter, Katherine Anne, 184

Powell, L. F., 176
Prokofiev, Sergei, 163
Proust, Marcel, 5, 160
Prouty, C. T., 88
pun, nature of the, 26–27, 38, 44, 76, 164

Quinn, Edward G., 173
Quintilian, 2

Rabelais, François, 4, 54, 149
Racine, Jean, 1
Ralegh, Sir Walter, 44
repetition, use in comedy of, 57–58, 76–77, 102, 170
Rich, Barnabe, 101, 172
Richard III, 169
Riche his Farewell to Militarie Profession, 101
Richter, Jean Paul, 158
Roberts, Warren, 159
Robertson, D. A., Jr., 161
romance, definition of, 46–47, 115, 167–68
romantic comedies, nature of Shakespeare's, 110–12
Romeo and Juliet, 74, 134, 142–43
Roper, William, 162
Rosalynde, 89
Rosencrantz and Guildenstern, 178
Rothwell, Fred, 158
Rowe, Nicholas, 167, 169

Santayana, George, quoted: 7–9, 10, 13–15, 25, 26, 46–47, 75, 125, 131, 133, 141, 151, 152–53, 154, 155, 156–57, 159, 162, 164, 167, 178, 179, 180–81, 182, 183–84; referred to: 11, 16, 104, 112, 160, 161, 183, 184, 185
Sartre, Jean Paul, 183
satiric, nature of the, 3, 21–23, 56, 63–64, 67, 114, 133
Second Shepherd's Play, The, 37
Sedgwick, G. G., 163
Seng, Peter, 170
Shaaber, M. A., 176

Shadwell, Thomas, 3
Shaw, Bernard, 2, 20, 43
Sherburn, George, 163, 168
Sidney, Sir Philip, 25, 32, 47, 164, 165
Simpson, Percy, 158
Singer, Irving, 160
Sir Gawain and the Green Knight, 47
Smith, J. C., 170
Somers, Sir George, 117
Sophocles, 30, 54
Spencer, Hazelton, 44, 167, 169
Spencer, Theodore, 169, 184
Spender, Stephen, 160–61
Spens, Janet, 161
Spenser, Edmund, 78
Spivack, Bernard, 179–80
Sprague, A. C., 175, 176
Stevens, Wallace, 184–85
Stoll, E. E., 52, 58, 127, 168, 175
Stoppard, Tom, 178
Strachey, Lytton, 179
Supposes, 39
Swift, Jonathan, 19, 21, 149, 181
Synge, J. M., 162

Taming of a Shrew, The, 38–40, 48–49
Taming of the Shrew, The, 36, 38–43, 48–49, 55, 73, 74
Tartuffe, 158
Tempest, The, 114, 116–24, 173
Terence, 37
Theobald, Lewis, 131
Theseus, Life of, 67
Thomas, Thomas, 165
Thurber, James, 54
Tillyard, E. M. W., 115–16, 161, 174
Titus Andronicus, 1, 169
To Be Young, Gifted, and Black, 182
Tractatus Coislinianus, 2
tragic, nature of the, 9–13, 16, 31 (tragedy defined), 71, 73–75, 116, 133–34 (heroically tragic),

139–42, 145–46, 161 (heroically tragic), 175–76, 177–78, 180, 182
tragicomedy, nature of, 115, 173
transvestism, comic use of, 96–97, 171. *See also* disguise
travesty, nature of, 169
Trick to Catch the Old One, A, 22
tricks, nature of. *See* jokes
Troilus and Cressida, 113–14
Twain, Mark, 4
Twelfth Night, 55, 77, 89, 101–10, 112, 113, 172
Two Gentlemen of Verona, The, 50–55, 62, 64, 72, 77, 168
Two Noble Kinsmen, The, 114, 124

Unterecker, John, 173

Vanbrugh, Sir John, 3
Vice, 34, 126, 134, 143, 175

Voltaire, François de, 4, 18

Waiting for Godot, 177
Walpole, Horace, 9, 10, 161
Ward, Douglas Turner, 182–83
Watts, Robert A., 179
Wellwarth, George E., 183
Welsford, Enid, 173
Willoughby, Edwin E., 162
Wilson, Edmund, 184
Wilson, John Dover, 166, 174
Wilson, Thomas, 159
Winter's Tale, The, 114, 116, 124
wit, nature of, 24–27, 29, 59–60, 63
Woolf, Virginia, 184
Worcester, David, 23–24, 147–49, 158, 163, 169, 181
Wycherley, William, 3

Yeats, William Butler, 112, 123, 173, 182